Electric Easy!

Cooking Under Pressure

101 Fast & Fabulous Recipes
for Today's Electric Pressure Cookers

by Alison DuBois Scutte

ELECTRIC EATS: COOKING UNDER PRESSURE! 101 FAST & FABULOUS RECIPES FOR TODAY'S ELECTRIC PRESSURE COOKERS!
WRITTEN BY ALISON DUBOIS SCUTTE
PUBLISHED BY JUMPSTART PRODUCTIONS INC. OLDSMAR, FL

ISBN 978-0-578-15436-7

FIRST PRINTING: APRIL 2015   15,000 COPIES
PRINTED IN CHINA

Contents

I. BEYOND THE MANUAL...
Tips & Tricks to Master your Electric PC

II. LET'S GET COOKING...
Recipes & Time Charts

Soups & Chili

Fresh Vegetables

Meat Lovers Entrées

- Recipes

Desserts

- Cooking Tips

- Recipes

Poached Pears pg 153

BEYOND THE MANUAL...

Wouldn't it be nice if product manuals gave you the inside skinny on using the (in this case) Pressure Cooker?!

I'm not saying that the Manual included with your cooker isn't loaded with information necessary for you to use the appliance correctly. It absolutley is, but...there is many little nuances and tips that will minimize the fallout meals during the learning curve! That's where my book comes in!

As a child I watched my Grandmother and Mother use Pressure Cookers and enjoyed the delicious meals and now, as an adult, I have worked professionally with pressure cookers for over 17 years and learned many tricks and time- saving techniques along the way! Most of my work with pressure cookers comes from writing and presenting demonstrations on live TV so timing and appearance is always important.

The next few pages are completely loaded with information that will give you a great foundation to create fabulous meals in less time than you imagine. However, if you only take away these 3 rules-of-thumb about electric pressure cooking, you will save your self time, frustration and messy cabinets!

BE PREPARED - The French would say Mise en Place which loosely means *Everything prepped, ready and in it's Place*. This is the most important habit you could adopt when using your Electric Pressure Cooker and I cannot stress how important it is to have everything ready BEFORE you plug in your pressure cooker!

The cooker gets hot quickly and will burn your first ingredients as you rush to measure liquid and seasonings. It takes much less time in the long run if you just go ahead and prepare/measure all of the veggies, meats, liquids, seasonings before you begin to cook.

WAIT FOR THE PRESSURE - After attaching the lid and setting the pressure regulator, remain in close proximity until pressure has been reached. Sometimes it is necessary to jiggle the exhaust valve or twist the lid to help the cooker achieve a proper seal. If you leave, and pressure is never achieved, your food will be under cooked and/ or burned.

USE A PAPER TOWEL WHEN EXHAUSTING PRESSURE - At no time should you restrict the air flow from the regulator when releasing the steam *BUT* there is nothing wrong with lightly draping a paper towel across the pressure regulator before exhausting the pressure to catch that first, oily, steam containing food particles. It's an easy step that you will be very glad you do!

These 3 tips will go along way to help you master electric pressure cooking but there is much more to know!

Pressure Cooking Basics

Always review your manufacturer's instruction manual prior to cooking the first time. It is very important to feel comfortable with your pressure cooker and be familiar with all of it's special features. Each individual cooker will have specific directions for bringing food up to pressure and releasing the pressure after the cooking time has elapsed; it is imperative that you follow the directions to ensure safe cooking.

If you misplace the manual, contact the manufacture for a replacement. Most manufacturers offer manuals (as well as recipes) in download-able files on their websites so take advantage of the service for worry-free cooking.

If you are using an older model and are unsure of the safety features, try to contact the manufacturer or ask your local librarian for a Pressure Cooker Cookbook that was published in approximately the same year the cooker was manufactured. If you cannot get a manual or instructions for safe usage, DO NOT USE THE COOKER!

Adapting your favorite (non-pressure cooker) Recipes

Everyone has his or her favorite recipes. Luckily, many can be adapted for use in your pressure cooker by following the rules and tips below along with the Time Charts listed within each food-specific recipe chapter.

- Recipes developed for Slow Cookers, Rice Cookers and Stove-Top methods usually work well in a Pressure Cooker while recipes prepared by Frying, Grilling or Baking do not generally yield positive results.
- Separate foods to be cooked according to size and length of cooking time needed. Many recipes will require that cooking be interrupted and additional fruits and vegetables added at a later time. Refer to the Cooking Time Chart so that all ingredients are cooked to their perfect doneness.
- Allow a minimum of ½ cup of liquid for every 10 minutes of cooking time. If time exceeds 30 minutes, add an additional ½ cup liquid to the recipe. Liquids include water, juice, stock, tomato sauce and purees but NOT oil.
- Never use less liquid than directed by your cooker's manual.
- Allow a minimum of 1 cup of liquid per 10 minutes of steaming time for vegetables and seafood.
- Decrease the amount of seasonings by ¼ as pressure cooking retains more of the foods natural flavor and seasonings are infused into the foods. Taste the food after cooking and add additional seasoning if needed.
- Refer to the food-specific sections following these General Rules for specific information on cooking and adapting recipes for meats and poultry, seafood, soups, vegetables, rice, grains and desserts.

To adapt the cooking time from traditional stove-top or oven methods to pressure cooking, you must be aware of the PSI of your Pressure Cooker. Consult your manual to find this information and then adjust your cooking times as follows:

- If using low pressure (5-8 PSI) reduce stated cooking time by ¼ (25%)
- If using medium pressure (10-12 PSI) reduce stated cooking time by 1/3 (33%)
- If using high pressure (13-15 PSI) reduce stated cooking time by ½ (50%)

You can always add cooking time if needed, but you can't un-cook overcooked foods!
I suggest you start by reducing the time by 30%, checking for doneness and then cooking longer if needed!

BROWNING & SEARING DIRECTIONS

Most recipes will instruct you to brown the foods first. Although optional, this step will not only enhance the flavor but will also yield a more attractive finished dish. To brown the food directly in the pressure cooker:

- Heat your Electric Pressure Cooker by selecting the preprogrammed "Brown" button or simply add 7 minutes to the Cook Time; 7 minutes is usually enough time to brown any of your foods but you can set it for longer if needed.
- Preheat a Tablespoon or two of oil before adding food to the pot..
- Turn the foods often to ensure even browning on all sides. When browning is complete remove large cuts of meat and immediately add a little (about ¼ cup) liquid and loosen the stuck on bits by scraping the bottom of the pan with a spatula or spoon. Not only will this greatly improve the richness of the flavor, it will keep burning at a minimum during the cooking process. Replace the meat or add the remaining ingredients.
- Remember to press Cancel before setting the actual Pressure Cooking time needed for your recipe.

STEAMING & ROASTING DIRECTIONS

- When cooking fresh vegetables or large cuts of meat in your pressure cooker, it is preferable to use a rack, trivet or steamer basket to keep the food off of the bottom of the pan.
- If cooking whole or cut up fresh vegetables, pour the desired liquid into the cooker first and then load the vegetables into the steamer basket (or oven safe dish) before lowering it into the cooker.
- If using a large cut of meat, follow the above directions under Browning & Sautéing. After you have deglazed the pan by adding your liquid, place a trivet or basket into the bottom of the cooker and position the meat on top. Add the remaining ingredients and continue to the next step.
- If your pressure cooker did not come with a trivet or rack, you may buy a fold-out steamer basket at any cooking store or use jar lids or rings distributed around the bottom of your cooker!

HOW TO LOAD THE INGREDIENTS

Never exceed the fill line of your pressure cooker. The cooker needs space to generate the necessary steam to promote pressure. Your cooker has been designed and tested to rapidly produce pressure in an allotted capacity; never overload your cooker!

HOW TO POSITION THE LID

- Attach and lock the lid onto the bottom of the cooker by following the directions for your specific cooker. However, before you position the lid it is best to always perform the following inspections to ensure the fastest, safest cooking.
- Check that the gasket is clean and inserted correctly into the lid. If the gasket seems dry, remove it from the lid, use mineral oil to lubricate it and then replace into proper position as directed in your cooker's manual.
- Inspect the exhaust valve to be sure there are no obstructions. Most cookers come with a tool for clearing the exhaust valve but if yours did not, use a METAL skewer to ensure the opening is free of debris. Never use a toothpick as it may break off in the valve opening!
- Adding 1 Tbsp. Oil to the liquid in the cooker will help the gasket stays lubricated and the exhaust valve clear.

How to use the Condensation Cup

This is a handy feature that keeps moisture from leaking out onto your counter top while cooking! If your pressure cooker came with a condensation cup, be sure it is in place before bringing the cooker up to pressure. Consult your manual for instructions on how to correctly attach the cup.

How to bring the cooker up to Pressure

- Since you are using an electric pressure cooker, all you need to do is set the exhaust valve to the "Airtight" or "closed" position, select your cooking time or preprogrammed time and press "Start"! Most electric cookers will automatically bring the cooker to pressure and then regulate it to keep the pressure at a steady level.
- If the Pressure Cooker is hissing, or any steam is escaping, it is NOT under full pressure. Jiggle the Exhaust valve until it is silent with no steam. If that doesn't help, you should remove the lid and check that the gasket is in place.
- Most Electric Pressure Cookers use a medium pressure (about 12 psi or pounds per square inch) and cannot be adjusted. If you are using a recipe that calls for low or high pressure please read below about adapting your recipe.

How to Release the Steam

When cooking is complete, press Cancel or unplug the cooker. The lid cannot be removed until the pressure is released. The steam should be released according to the manufactures directions and the type of food being cooked; see the Cooking Time Chart for suggested release methods. There are three general methods to releasing the steam:

- Quick Release Method
  - Push, turn or press the release valve into the "open" position. You may do this in bursts or in one continual motion but BE CAREFUL AS STEAM IS HOT!!
  - Quick releasing usually takes 30-45 seconds and can be useful for recipes that may over cook or need to have other ingredients added. There are foods, however, like rice, grains and beans that should never be Quick Released but work well with the Cold Water Release Method.
  - Although you DO NOT want to block the steam as it is being released, I loosely hold a paper towel over the vent. This captures the oils and food particles that may be expelled during steam release.
- Cold Release Method - For use with Stovetop Cookers only!
  - Place your non-electric cooker in the sink under a stream of cold running water. This works well for foods such as rice, grains and beans that have a lot of foam as well as for soups and other foods that contain mostly liquid.
  - Once the pressure indicator drops to normal, the cooker can be removed from the sink and opened. This method usually takes 4-5 minutes.
- Natural Release Method
  - As the name indicates, this method allows the cooker to cool at its own pace and release the steam naturally. You can however, help it along by placing the cooker away from heat and laying a damp towel over the cooker.
  - Make sure that the electric cooker does not automatically go to "keep warm" or this process will take much longer!

- This is the ideal method for rice, large cuts of meat, cheesecakes and desserts as well as stews and other dishes that benefit from longer cooking times.
- This method takes anywhere from 5-15 minutes depending on the capacity of the food inside of the cooker.

Note: If you have released the pressure but the lid will not open, it means that the cooker is under a vapor lock or vacuum lock. If this happens, unlock the lid, turn the exhaust valve to the open position and bring the cooker back to a low, non-pressurized heat for a couple of minutes. The lid should come off easily at this point.

SAFETY TIP: Always open the lid **AWAY** from your face!

CLEANING AND MAINTAINING YOUR PRESSURE COOKER

Keeping your pressure cooker clean and maintained is instrumental to safe cooking and will extend the life of your cooker so you will have years of problem-free cooking. Here are a few instructions and tips:

- Never put your pressure cooker lid in the dishwasher! Hand wash only and dry thoroughly before storing.
- Remove the insert from electric pressure cookers, wash and dry thoroughly and wipe inside the cooker with a damp cloth before reinserting the removable pot.
- Empty and wash the Condensation Cup (if applicable). Dry and store inside cooker to prevent it from being knocked off and lost while storing.
- Store accessories, manuals and plugs inside the cooker so they are not misplaced.
- Store the unit with the lid inverted, not in the locked position. This will prevent odors from being trapped inside the cooker.
- Always check that the gasket is clean and inserted correctly into the lid. If the gasket seems dry, remove it from the lid, use mineral oil to lubricate it and then replace it into proper position as directed in your cooker's manual. Properly maintained, the gasket should last about 150 uses.
- Before and after each use, inspect the exhaust valve to be sure there are no obstructions. Some lids have a snap-on screen on the inside of the lid to prevent clogs. Be sure to remove this to clean exhaust valve. Most cookers come with a tool for clearing the exhaust valve but if yours did not, use a metal skewer to ensure the opening is free of debris. DO NOT use a toothpick as it may break off inside of the valve.
- Never place the lid on a hot stove or over a burner as it may damage the gasket. If the Gasket is holding odors, place into hot white vinegar for 5-10 minutes. Remove, wash as usual, dry and replace inside the lid. Remember to oil it before it's next use.

Let's Get Cooking!
Recipes for Electric PC's

Alison DuBois Scutte
On-set at HSN with the Elite Pressure Cooker- 2010

My motivation for writing this book was to help the tens of thousands of you who have purchased Electric Pressure Cookers after watching TV shopping presentations and infomercials, only to be disappointed once you started using it. If you were using an older Pressure Cooker cookbook, it's no wonder your foods never seemed to be cooked as well as the food looked on TV! It's NOT your fault and it's NOT the PC's fault... it's the book you are using!

Most cookbooks written for pressure cookers are actually written for stove-top cookers, not electric. Does it make a difference? Absolutely! Stove-top versions can cook foods at 15 psi while the majority of Electric versions max out at 12 psi. That makes a huge difference when it comes to cooking times. Now that you have the right book, you should have better results.

In fact, the actual recipes that are used in many of the presentations on the shopping channels and infomercials can be found right here in this book.

Thanks...to my husband Al for his encouragement, for roughing it on his own while I was glued to my computer for the last few months and for his superb photography skills! Thanks also to Katie for giving me the push I needed to finally write this book! Finally, my special thanks goes out to all of you TV shoppers who continue to write and share your cooking experiences (good and bad) with me. It keeps me on my "culinary toes", helps me continue to develop new recipes and WOW demos for on-air presentations and warms my heart to hear that some of my recipes have woven their way into the fabric of your family. I hope that these new recipes bring much joy to your family dinner table for years to come and look I forward to hearing your stories! Happy Cooking!

Alison D. Scutte

11

About Cooking Soups and Stocks

- Soups with ingredients that tend to foam, like dried beans and split peas, could cause the exhaust valve to clog. To prevent this, add 1 Tbs. Oil to each cup of dried beans or other foam-inducing ingredient.

- Due to the lack of evaporation when using a pressure cooker, reduce the liquid required in standard recipes by 1 cup. Reduce the liquid further if necessary to remain BELOW the Max fill line of your pressure cooker!

- Soups will take approximately 20 minutes to come to pressure due to the large liquid ratio.

- Refer to the time chart when making soups containing mixtures of meats, beans and vegetables. The vegetables will overcook if added at the same time as the meat!

- Season lightly as pressure cookers intensify the flavors. You can adjust later if necessary.

- Release pressure using the Natural Release Method or the Cold Water Method only.

SOUP & CHILI

Slow Cook Fast!!

Soups, stews and chili usually require all-day slow cooking for rich, flavorful results. By using your Pressure Cooker, you will get the same slow-cooked flavors in a fraction of the time! Try a few of the recipes in this Chapter and you'll be hooked!

Great Northern Bean Soup

Prep Time: 70 minutes   Ready in: 45 minutes   Yield: 6-8 servings

INGREDIENTS
16 oz. dried great northern beans
10 Cups water
2 Tbsp Oil
8 oz. ham cubes
7 Cups water
1 small onion; chopped
1 Cup celery ribs and leaves; sliced
1 Cup carrots; chopped2 bay leaves
1 tsp Coarse ground black pepper
2 tsp Kosher salt
3 dashes Tabasco
1 Cup instant mashed potato flakes

DIRECTIONS
1. Place your pressure cooker on a level surface, and plug the unit in.
2. Add dried beans and 10 cups water into pressure pan. Set Cook Time to 4 minutes and Press Start.
3. Attach and lock the lid of your pressure cooker; set the pressure control to Air Tight (closed). When cooking is complete, press Cancel to turn off the keep warm feature and let rest 1 hour.
4. Remove lid; drain and rinse beans. Leave in the colander until needed.
5. Wash and dry the pan and place back into the base. Set Cook Time for 30 min and press Start.
6. Add oil and when hot, add ham cubes and brown lightly for about 1 minute.
7. Add the water and scrape the bottom of the pan with a spatula to loosen any ham bits. Add the rinsed beans and the remaining ingredients, except for potato flakes, and stir well.
8. Replace lid, close the exhaust valve and let cook the 30 minutes.
9. When cooking time has elapsed, press Cancel to turn off the Keep Warm setting and let release pressure naturally until you can safely remove lid.
10. Check to make sure that the beans are tender; if not, replace lid and cook another 10 minutes.
11. When beans are tender, stir in the potato flakes.
12. Cover with glass lid (or pressure cooker lid with valve on Exhaust) and allow to cook on low 5 minutes. If a thicker soup is desired, use ½ cup more potato flakes.

Split Pea & Ham Soup

Prep Time: 70 minutes   Ready in: 45 minutes   Yield: 6-8 servings

INGREDIENTS

1 lb green split peas, picked over, rinsed and drained
2 large smoked ham hocks
1 small onion; chopped
1 Cup celery ribs and leaves; sliced
1 Cup carrots; chopped

4 sprigs fresh thyme
1 bay leaf
6 cups low-sodium chicken broth or stock, water or a combination of both
Kosher salt and freshly ground black pepper

DIRECTIONS

1. Place your pressure cooker on a level surface, and plug the unit in.
2. Drain and rinse peas. Leave in the colander until needed.
3. Set Cook Time for 30 min and press Start.
4. Add oil and when hot, add ham cubes and brown lightly for about 1 minute.
5. Add the water and scrape the bottom of the pan with a spatula to loosen any ham bits. Add the rinsed peas and the remaining ingredients.
6. Attach lid, close the exhaust valve to Air Tight and let cook the 30 minutes.
7. When cooking time has elapsed, cancel the Keep Warm setting and let release pressure naturally until you can safely remove lid. Remove bay leaf and thyme stems and discard.
8. Check to make sure that the beans are tender; if not, replace lid and cook another 10 minutes.
9. Remove 1/2 Cup of the split peas and mash them in a blender or chopper. Stir back into the soup.
10. Cover with glass lid (or pressure cooker lid with valve on Exhaust) and allow to cook on low 5 minutes. If a thicker soup is desired, use ½ cup more potato flakes.

ULTIMATE CHILI WITH MEAT & BEANS

Prep Time: 15 minutes   Ready in: 45 minutes   Yield: 10-12 servings

INGREDIENTS
1 Tbsp vegetable oil
1 1/4 lb. ground turkey (you may use all turkey or all beef if desired)
1 lb. ground beef; at least 80% lean
      (you may use all turkey or all beef if desired)
1 medium onion chopped; about 1 C
1 medium green bell pepper coarsely chopped; about 1 C
1/2 tsp garlic powder
3 tsp ground cumin
1 tsp salt
3 Tbsp chili powder
1 29-oz can tomato sauce
1 29-oz can crushed tomatoes
1 1/2 Cup water; divided between the tomato cans to swish
1 Cup V-8 Juice spicy hot flavor
1 lb dried kidney beans; washed and picked over for broken beans or pebbles

Optional Toppings: Shredded Cheddar cheese, Light sour cream, chopped onion, pickled jalapeño pepper slices

DIRECTIONS
1. Place pressure cooker on a level surface, insert the pan and plug in.
2. Set Cook Time for 35 minutes and press Start.
3. Add the oil, ground turkey and ground beef to pan. Begin browning the meat, stirring often. When meat begins to brown, stir in the chopped onion and pepper along with the seasonings. Stir and cook about 1 minute.
4. Stir in the crushed tomatoes and the tomato sauce. Pour 3/4 C water into each can and swish around to capture the remaining tomato and then pour into the pot.
5. Add the spicy V-8 juice and the washed kidney beans.
6. Attach the lid and set regulator valve to Air Tight (closed).
7. When cooking time has elapsed, unplug the pressure cooker and let the pressure release naturally.
8. Carefully open the lid, stir and taste the beans for doneness. If more time is needed, set the pressure cooker to Keep Warm and simmer until done. Cover with the pressure lid (on Exhaust) or with the glass lid.

Dress Up your Chili!

Chili is a favorite PC recipe because you can make it with dried beans! Not only a healthy and delicious choice but a very cost efferctive way to serve a large group!

To keep it interesting, think outside the bowl and serve your chili over...

tortilla chips
hot baked potatoes
hot dogs
Southwestern Salads
elbow macaroni
Fritos® corn chips

And top it with:

shredded cheeses
sour cream
diced onions
jalapeno pepper

WHITE CHILI

Prep Time: 15 minutes   Ready in: 40 minutes   Yield: 8-10 servings

INGREDIENTS

2 lbs boneless skinless chicken breast
2 large onions; chopped
5 cloves garlic; chopped
1 Tbsp olive oil
¼ Cup lime juice & 1 tsp lime zest
Red pepper flakes
2 16-oz cans great northern beans
1 (4 oz) can of green chilies
1 Tbsp cumin
1 tsp salt
1-2 tsp cayenne pepper depending on heat desired
3-4 Cups chicken broth
Finely Shredded Monterey or Cheddar Cheese (optional)
Sour cream (optional)

DIRECTIONS

1. Place your pressure cooker on a level surface, and plug the unit in.
2. Set Cook Time to 20 min or select the Chicken setting; press Start.
3. When the pot is hot add 1 Tbsp of the oil. Add the chicken pieces and cook until they are beginning to brown.
4. Stir in the onions and cook until they are soft. Add garlic, lime juice, lime zest and a generous pinch of crushed red peppers.
5. Add the beans, chilies, cumin and salt; stir well. Add your desired amount of chicken stock based on your preferred thickness of the chili.
6. Attach the lid and set the pressure valve to Air Tight.
7. When the cooking time has elapsed, press Cancel to turn off the Keep Warm setting and allow cooker to sit 10 minutes before manually releasing the remaining pressure. Carefully open the lid away from you and stir the chili well.
8. Serve with shredded Monterey Jack or Cheddar cheese and a dollop of sour cream for an extra-yummy treat!

TO MAKE THIS CHILI USING DRIED BEANS, JUST ADD 1 CUP LIQUID AND INCREASE THE COOKING TIME TO 40 MINUTES!

CHICKEN TORTILLA SOUP

Prep Time: 15 minutes   Ready in: 35 minutes   Yield: 6-8 servings

INGREDIENTS

1 Store-bought Rotisserie Chicken; or the meat from 1 3-lb cooked chicken
2 Tbsp Olive Oil
½ Cup sweet yellow onion; chopped
1/2 Cup crushed tortilla chips
1 15 ¼ -oz can whole kernel corn; drained
1 ½ tsp ground Cumin
1 4-oz. Can chopped Green Chilies
1 15 ½ -oz can black beans; top liquid drained
1 28-oz can crushed tomatoes
6 Cups chicken broth
2 Tbsp Better than Bouillon Chicken Base
1 small pinch dried Chipotle Chili Pepper
Avocado, Sour Cream and Tortilla Chips as desired

DIRECTIONS

1. Remove the meat from the rotisserie chicken; discard bones and skin. Chop meat into bite-sized pieces. Set aside.
2. Place your pressure cooker on a level surface, and plug the unit in.
3. Set Cook Time to 20 min or select the Soup/Stew" setting; press Start.
4. Add the olive oil and chopped onion to the pot and sauté for about 2 minutes, stirring often. Add the corn chips and cook another minute. Add the corn and cumin and cook another minute.
5. Add the remaining ingredients, stirring after each ingredient.
6. Attach the lid and set the pressure valve to Air Tight.
7. When cooking time has elapsed, cancel the Keep Warm feature and allow the pressure release naturally.
8. To serve: Ladle the soup into a bowl. Top with a dollop of sour cream, avocado pieces and crumbled tortilla chips if desired.

TIP: USE BONELESS, SKINLESS CHICKEN BREAST TO ELIMINATE THE BONING PROCESS. AFTER COOKING, CUT OR SHRED THE BREASTS ADD TO THE BROTH WITH THE VEGGIES AND CONTINUE AS DIRECTED.

OKTOBERFEST BEER CHEESE SOUP

Prep Time: 15 minutes   Ready in: 30 minutes   Yield: 8-10 servings

INGREDIENTS
1 stick butter (1/2 C)
1 medium sweet yellow onion; minced (about 1 C)
1 medium carrot; finely diced (about 1 C)
2 stalks celery; finely diced (about 1/2 C)
1/2 tsp celery salt
1/2 tsp paprika
1/2 tsp dry mustard
1/2 tsp salt
1/3 Cup plus 2 Tbs. Flour (1/2 Cup for dip)
1 bottle dark beer (I used Samuel Adams Oktoberfest Beer)
5 Cups chicken broth (3 Cups for dip)
12-oz sharp cheddar cheese; shredded
4-oz cream cheese; cut into pieces
1 Cup half and half
1/2 tsp Tabasco

DIRECTIONS
1. Place your pressure cooker on a level surface, and plug the unit in.   Set Cook Time to 20 min; press Start.
2. Add the cold butter to the pot at the same time as the onion, carrots and celery. When the butter has completely melted and the veggies are sautéing sprinkle in the paprika, dry mustard, salt and flour. Stir well and cook another minute.
3. Pour beer into the mixture, stirring constantly and cook until boiling. Stir in the chicken broth.
4. Attach lid and set regulator valve to Air Tight (closed).
5. When cooking time has elapsed, press Cancel and release the pressure manually or allow it to release naturally.
6. Remove the lid and stir. Use an immersion blender directly into the pressure pot to puree the veggies until smooth or process in a blender in batches. Turn the pressure cooker to Keep Warm.
7. Add the cheeses and stir until completely melted. Add the Tabasco Sauce. Finally, add the half and half, stir and cook until heated through. Do not let it boil!
8. Serve hot in bowls. Offer Tabasco Sauce along with a variety of toppings like hard pretzel sticks, garlic croutons, cauliflower or broccoli florets and sliced green apples.

Everyone loves Beer Cheese Fondue!

If you prefer a thick, fondue rather than a thinner soup, simply use the quantities listed in blue (left) and you'll turn this incredibly yummy soup into a party-pleasing dip served with:
pretzel sticks,
apple sticks,
carrots and
cauliflower!

Chicken & Sausage Gumbo

Prep Time: 30 minutes   Ready in: 40 minutes   Yield: 8-10 servings

INGREDIENTS
1/4 Cup vegetable oil; divided
1 lb. Andouille sausage; cut into 1/4" thick slices
2 tsp Cajun seasoning
2 lb. chicken thighs; skin removed
3 Tbsp flour
1 very large yellow onion; coarsely chopped
2 medium red bell peppers; seeds and membrane removed and coarsely chopped
1 28-oz can crushed tomato
1 28-oz can petite diced tomatoes
2 Cups chicken broth
1 Tbsp (heaping) file seasoning
1/4 tsp cayenne pepper
2 bay leaves
1 16-oz bag frozen cut okra
salt and pepper to taste
Tabasco Sauce, optional
4 Cups cooked, hot white rice

DIRECTIONS
1. Wash and pat dry the chicken thighs. Sprinkle with the Cajun seasoning.
2. Place the pressure cooker on a level surface, insert the pressure pan and plug in.
3. Set Cook Time for 25 minutes and press Start.
4. Add 3 Tbsp of the oil to the pan. Add the sausage and cook for 5 min or until well browned; remove and drain on paper towels.
5. Cook the chicken in batches, to prevent over-crowding, 3 minutes per side or until brown; drain on paper towels with the sausage until needed.
6. Add the remaining oil along with the flour to the pan and cook for 4-5 minutes or until the mixture is dark brown.
7. In the meantime, place the peppers and onion into a microwave safe dish with 2 Tablespoons of water, cover

loosely with a damp paper towel and microwave for 3 minutes. Carefully remove from microwave and stir into the browned flour until coated.

8. Add the garlic, tomatoes, water, file, cayenne and bay leaves. Stir well and then add the sausage and chicken back into the mixture.
9. Attach the lid and set the exhaust valve to Air Tight (closed).
10. While Gumbo is under pressure, cook 4 cups of long grain rice, according to directions and set aside.
11. When the cooking time has elapsed in the pressure cooker, unplug and let rest for 5 minutes. Placing a paper towel over the vent and release the remaining pressure.
12. Carefully open the lid and stir in the okra. Set the Cook Time for 4 minutes, reattach lid and return valve to the closed position. Press Start.
13. When the cooking time has elapsed, let the pressure release naturally for about 10 minutes. When it is safe to open the lid, use tongs and remove the chicken to a cutting board, close the cooker lid, with the valve open and let simmer on Keep Warm.
14. When the chicken is cool enough to handle, remove the chicken from the pot. When it is cool enough to handle, remove the meat from the bones, shred the meat and return to the pot; discard bones.
15. Continue cooking on Keep Warm until the chicken is reheated throughout
16. To serve, place about 1/4 C rice into the bottom of a bowl or cup and ladle 1 Cup gumbo over the top. Taste and add Tabasco sauce if desired.

NOTE: IF YOU CANNOT FIND THE ANDOUILLE SAUSAGE YOU MAY SUBSTITUTE SMOKED SAUSAGE INSTEAD.

CREAM OF MUSHROOM SOUP

Prep Time: 15 minutes   Ready in: 30 minutes   Yield: 8-10 servings

INGREDIENTS
4 Tbsp Butter
2 shallots; finely minced
1 lb. sliced mushrooms
1 tsp salt
½ tsp ground black pepper
1 tsp tarragon flakes or 3 Tbsp fresh Tarragon leaves
¼ tsp. ground thyme or 1 Tbsp fresh thyme leaves
4 Cups chicken broth
1 Cup water
¼ Cup heavy cream

DIRECTIONS
1. Place pressure cooker on a level surface, insert pressure pan and plug in.
2. Set Cook Time to 15 minutes and press Start.
3. Add butter and when melted, add Shallots and mushrooms and gently sauté until tender and lightly browned. Add chicken broth, water, potatoes, tarragon, thyme, salt and pepper.
4. Attach lid and set the regulator valve to Air Tight (closed).
5. When cooking time has elapsed, press Cancel to stop the Keep Warm function. Wait 10 minutes before releasing any remaining pressure.
6. Turn the pressure cooker to Keep Warm Using an Immersion Blender directly into the pressure pot, process the mushrooms until you reach your preferred consistency; chunky to smooth.
7. Adjust seasonings as needed and add cream. Heat until mixture is just warmed throughout. Do not boil!

**NOTE: FRESH OR DRIED, DO NOT OMIT THE TARRAGON IN THIS DISH.
IT ADDS THAT LITTLE FLAVOR THAT KEEPS THEM GUESSING YOUR RECIPE!**

TOMATO BASIL SOUP
Prep Time: 5 minutes   Ready in: 25 minutes   Yield: 8-10 servings

INGREDIENTS
2 28-oz. Cans whole peeled tomatoes
1 Cup vegetable stock
1 Tbsp olive oil
2 cloves garlic; finely chopped
1 medium onion; chopped
¼ tsp dried thyme
½ Cup fresh basil leaves; washed and thinly sliced; save 3-4 whole leaves for garnish
Pinch of sugar
salt and pepper to taste
1/3 Cup Half n Half

DIRECTIONS
1. Place pressure cooker on a level surface, insert pressure pan and plug in.
2. Set Cook Time to 10 minutes and press Start.
3. Add oil and when hot, add onion and gently sauté until tender.
4. Add garlic, thyme and basil and sauté another minute.
5. Add the tomatoes, water and a pinch of sugar.
6. Attach lid and set the regulator valve to Air Tight (closed).
7. When cooking time has elapsed, press Cancel to stop the Keep Warm function. Wait 5 minutes before releasing any remaining pressure.
8. Turn the pressure cooker to Keep Warm. Using an Immersion Blender directly into the pressure pot, process the tomatoes until smooth or to your preferred consistency.
9. Stir in the cream and heat through but do not boil!

TV Tidbit: Tomato soup is a widely used demo on TV for pressure cookers, expensive blenders and for immersion blenders! Its easy and delicious but be sure to add a small dollop of sour cream or a swirl of cream and a basil leaf as garnish so it looks TV ready!

French Onion Soup

Prep Time: 10 minutes   Ready in: 45 minutes   Yield: 10-12 servings

INGREDIENTS

2 tsp olive oil

¾-1 pound prime rib or T-Bone steak

2 Tbsp Worcestershire sauce

salt and pepper

½ Cup water

2 very large Spanish or Vidalia onions, about 1 ½ pounds; quartered and sliced ¼ " thick

4 Tbsp butter

1 Tbsp olive oil

2 Tbsp flour

7 ½ Cups water

3 Tbsp Better-Than-Bullion Beef Base

1 round slice Provolone Cheese for each serving

Parmesan cheese; finely shredded

Garlic Croutons - store bought or homemade as directed

DIRECTIONS

1. Place the pressure cooker on a level surface, insert the pressure pan and plug in. Set Cook time to 15 minutes or choose the preprogrammed Meat button; press Start.

2. Add 2 tsp olive oil. Lightly salt and pepper both sides of the steak and, when oil is hot, place steak into the pan and sear on both sides. Sprinkle the Worcestershire sauce over the steak and ½ cup water around the steak.

3. Attach lid and set the regulator valve to Air Tight (closed). When cooking time has elapsed, manually release the pressure and carefully open the lid. Transfer steak onto a plate; when cool enough to handle, trim all fat and cut steak into small bite-sized pieces.

4. Set Cook Time to 10 min and press Start. When liquid in pot begins to boil, stir in the remaining Worcestershire sauce, the Beef Base and the water. Bring liquid to a boil and cook 3-4 minutes, stirring often. Press Cancel and carefully pour the liquid into a bowl or measuring cup and set aside.

5. Wash, dry and replace the pressure pot into the cooker. Set Cook Time to 10 minutes; press Start. Add 4 Tbsp butter and 1 Tbsp olive oil into the pan and when hot, add sliced onions. Cook 2-3 minutes, stirring constantly until onions begin to brown. Add the steak to the onion. Sprinkle flour over the meat and onions; gently toss and cook until heated through. Slowly pour in the broth and stir well.

6. Attach lid and set the regulator valve to Air Tight (closed). When cooking time has elapsed, manually release the pressure and carefully open the lid. Assemble & Serve!

To make the Croutons - Melt the butter with the garlic clove in a small saucepan over low heat and let sit for 5 minutes. Brush both sides of 6-7 slices of French baguette bread with the butter and place into 250F oven for 10 minutes on each side.

To assemble & serve - Place 3-4 croutons into the bottom of each oven-proof soup crock. Ladle soup over croutons. Top with a slice of Provolone and a generous sprinkling of the shredded Parmesan cheese. Place under broiler until cheeses begin to melt and brown.

Beef, Barley & Vegetable Soup
Prep Time: 10 minutes   Ready in: 1 hour   Yield: 8-10 servings

INGREDIENTS
2 Tbsp vegetable oil
1 medium onion; diced
2 stalks celery; sliced
1 clove garlic; minced
3 Tbsp Better than Bouillon Beef or 6 beef bouillon cubes
6 Cups water
2 medium bay leaves
2 lbs. Beef stew or soup pieces
½ Cup medium barley (uncooked)
1 14.5-oz. Can petite diced tomatoes
1 9-oz. Package frozen mixed vegetables

DIRECTIONS
1. Place the pressure cooker on a level surface, insert the pressure pan and plug in.
2. Set Cook Time to 20 minutes and press Start.
3. Add the oil to the cooker. When the oil is hot, add the onion, celery and garlic and sauté for 3 - 4 minutes.
4. Add 1 Cup of the water and the bullion; stir until bouillon is dissolved.
5. Add the beef, the remaining 5 Cups water and the bay leaves.
6. Attach lid and set the regulator valve to Air Tight (closed).
7. When cooking time has elapsed, press Cancel to stop the Keep Warm function. Wait 5 minutes before releasing any remaining pressure.
8. Add the barley and the can of tomatoes. Reattach lid, set valve to Air Tight. Set Cook Time for 20 minutes, press Start.
9. When cooking time has elapsed, press Cancel to stop the Keep Warm function. Wait 5 minutes before releasing any remaining pressure.
10. Carefully open the lid and stir in the frozen vegetables.
11. Reattach lid, set valve to Air Tight. Set Cook Time for 2 minutes, press Start.
12. When cook time is up, unplug machine and let pressure release naturally.

NOTE: Additional water may be needed if soup becomes too thick upon standing.

POTATO LEEK SOUP

Prep Time: 15 minutes   Ready in: 30 minutes   Yield: 8-10 servings

INGREDIENTS
½ stick butter
1 large leek; green tops removed
8 medium white potatoes, peeled and quartered4 Cups chicken broth
1 Cups water
1 tsp Salt
½ tsp Ground black pepper
½ cup heavy cream

DIRECTIONS
1. Thinly slice the white only of the leek; you should end up with about 1-1 ¼ cups.
2. Place pressure cooker on a level surface, insert pressure pan and plug in.
3. Set Cook Time to 15 minutes and press Start.
4. Add butter and when melted, add leeks and gently sauté until tender but not browned. Add chicken broth, water, potatoes, salt and pepper.
5. Attach lid and set the regulator valve to Air Tight (closed).
6. When cooking time has elapsed, press Cancel to stop the Keep Warm function. Wait 10 minutes before releasing any remaining pressure.
7. Turn the pressure cooker to Keep Warm Using an Immersion Blender directly into the pressure pot, process potatoes and leeks until completely smooth.
8. Adjust seasonings as needed and add cream. Heat until mixture is just warmed throughout. Do not boil!
9. Serve hot with fresh ground black pepper.

Tuscan Bean Soup

Prep Time: 10 minutes   Ready in: 45 minutes   Yield: 10-12 servings

INGREDIENTS
6 Italian Sausages; about 1 ¼ to 1 ½ pounds
1 Cup water
1 4-oz. piece of salt pork
2 Tbsp olive oil
2 cloves garlic; chopped
1 medium onion; chopped
2 celery ribs; thickly sliced
1 carrot; thinly sliced
4 Cups chicken stock or broth
1 28-oz. Can Italian peeled tomatoes; drained and chopped
1 head escarole or collard greens; leaves cut into 3 inch pieces
3 19-oz. Can Cannellini beans (white kidney beans)
2 15.5-oz. Can dark red kidney beans
salt and pepper, hot pepper flakes & grated Romano cheese as desired

DIRECTIONS
1. Place the pressure cooker on a level surface, insert the pressure pan and plug in.
2. Prick sausages all over with a fork. Place into the pressure pan along with 1 cup of water.
3. Attach lid and set the regulator valve to Air Tight (closed). Set Cook Time to 10 minutes and press Start.
4. When cooking time has elapsed, manually release the pressure and carefully open the lid. Transfer the sausages to a plate and drain the liquid from the pot.
5. Replace the pot into the cooker, set Cook Time to 10 minutes and press Start.
6. Add the oil to the cooker. When the oil is hot, add the salt pork, onion, celery, carrots and garlic and sauté for 3 - 4 minutes. Add the chicken stock, tomatoes, greens and beans. Stir well.
7. Chop the Italian Sausages into bite-sized pieces and add to mixture.
8. Attach lid and set the regulator valve to Air Tight (closed).
9. When cooking time has elapsed, press Cancel to stop the Keep Warm function. Let pressure release naturally.
10. Remove and discard the salt pork. Stir well, taste and adjust salt and pepper as needed.
11. Serve in bowls; offering hot pepper flakes and grated Romano cheese on the side.
        NOTE: TO USE DRIED BEANS, CONSULT THE TIME CHART AND PRECOOK THE BEANS BEFORE GOING ON TO STEP 2.

Chicken Noodle Soup

Prep Time: 15 minutes   Ready in: 45-50 minutes   Yield: 8 servings

INGREDIENTS
3-4 lb. whole fryer chicken
2 Tbsp olive oil
1 Tbsp butter
1 medium onion; coarsely chopped
6 Cups canned chicken broth
1 ¼ Cup chopped celery
1 ¼ Cup chopped carrots
2 tsp kosher salt
1 tsp ground black pepper
1 tsp thyme
1 Tbsp dried parsley
8 oz. wide egg noodles

DIRECTIONS
1. Wash, pat dry, lightly salt and pepper chicken inside and out.
2. Place your pressure cooker on a level surface, insert the pressure pot, and plug the unit in.
3. Set cook time to 10 minutes or select the preprogrammed Brown button; press Start.
4. When the pan is hot add the olive oil and butter followed by the add onion; sauté until lightly brown.
5. Add chicken broth, salt, pepper, thyme and dried parsley. Stir well and then place chicken into pot.
6. Attach and lock the lid of your pressure cooker; set the pressure control to Air Tight (closed).
7. Press the Cancel button and reset the Cook Time for 15 minutes; or press the preprogrammed Chicken button; press Start.
8. When cooking is complete, press Cancel to turn off the Keep Warm feature and let rest 5 minutes before manually   exhausting the pressure. Once the pressure has been released, carefully open the lid and stir well.
9. Remove chicken and allow to cool enough to handle. Remove the bones and skin from the chicken and discard. Strain any unsavory bits from the broth and discard.
10. Cut chicken into bite size pieces and return to the broth. Set Cook Time to 6 minutes; press Start.
11. Allow the mixture to come to a gentle boil and add the rest of the ingredients, including the noodles. Stir well.
12. Replace pressure lid, set exhaust valve to Air Tight.
13. When time has elapsed, manually release the pressure until you can remove lid.
14. Check the doneness of the noodles and serve immediately.
15. If more time is needed, cover and cook on Keep Warm until the noodles are tender. Serve hot with crackers.

About Cooking Vegetables

- Vegetables cooked in the Pressure Cooker are second only to raw when it comes to nutrients! The airtight environment will re-infuse the vital nutrients back into the foods along with any seasonings added. Be careful not to over-season.

- Cut vegetables into uniform sized pieces to ensure even cooking. If cooking a variety of vegetables, cut them into pieces large to small in order of their cooking times; for example cut pieces of squash and zucchini into 1 inch pieces and carrots into ¼-inch pieces if cooking for the same length of time!

- Use a steam basket whenever possible to keep the vegetables above the water; this will prevent burning as well as help retain vital nutrients.

- Use the minimum amount of water or stock as directed by your pressure cooker's manual.

- If cooking frozen vegetables, use the same amount of water as directed on the package, but cook for the same amount of time as you would for fresh vegetables.

- As in all pressure cooking, the cook time starts WHEN PRESSURE IS REACHED; set your timer correctly to avoid overcooking! You can always add more time in necessary so when in doubt choose the quickest time.

- Use the Quick Release Method for releasing the steam to avoid over cooking the vegetables.

- Refer to the following cooking time charts and have fun experimenting with different liquids. Try broth, wine and fruit juices for bold new flavors!

Fresh Vegetables

Agave Carrots
Artichokes
Asparagus
Brussels Sprouts
Buttery Corn-on-the-Cob
Cauliflower
Cheesy Garlic Smashed Potatoes
Cranberry Stuffing
Parsley Potatoes
Perfect Green Beans
Red Cabbage Kraut
Sweet Potato Mash
Swiss Chard

Vegetable Cooking Time Charts

All cook times are based on a 12psi Electric Pressure Cooker. To adjust see Adapting Your Recipes in Chapter 1.

VEGETABLE	MAX QUANTITY	MIN LIQUID	MIN COOK TIME	RELEASE METHOD
Artichoke, large whole	6-8	1 Cup	13-14	quick or natural
Artichoke, medium whole	8-10	1 Cup	11-12	quick or natural
Artichoke, small whole	Half-full	1 Cup	9-10	quick or natural
Artichoke, hearts	3 Cups	1 Cup	5-6	quick
Asparagus, fine, whole	1-2 lb.	3/4 Cup	3-4	quick
Asparagus, thick, whole	1-2 lb.	3/4 Cup	5-6	quick
Beans, green, whole (fresh or frozen)	1-2 lb.	3/4 Cup	4-5	quick
Beets, 1/4" (5 mm) slices	2 Cups	3/4 Cup	8	quick or natural
Beets, medium whole, peeled	Half-full	3/4 Cup	13-14	quick or natural
Beets, large whole, peeled	Half-full	1 Cup	20-22	quick or natural
Broccoli, florets or spears	Half-full	3/4 Cup	3	quick
Brussels Sprouts, whole	1-2 lb.	3/4 Cup	8-9	quick
Cabbage, red or green, quartered	Half-full	1 Cup	5	quick
Carrots, 1/4" slices	2 Cups	3/4 Cup	3-4	quick
Carrots, 1" chunks or whole baby	2 Cups	3/4 Cup	5-6	quick
Cauliflower, florets	Half-full	3/4 Cup	5-6	quick
Cauliflower, whole head	1-2 lb.	3/4 Cup	7-8	quick
Collard Greens	3/4 full	1 Cup	6	quick
Corn on the Cob	6-8	3/4 Cup	7-8	quick or natural

Vegetable Cooking Time Charts

All cook times are based on a 12psi Electric Pressure Cooker. To adjust see Adapting Your Recipes in Chapter 1.

VEGETABLE	MAX QUANTITY	MIN LIQUID	MIN COOK TIME	RELEASE METHOD
Eggplant, 1" chunks or slices	2 Cups	3/4 Cup	4	quick
Endive or Escarole, coarsely chopped	3/4 full	1 Cup	4	quick
Kale	3/4 full	1 Cup	4	quick
Leeks, white parts cut in 1" rings	Half-full	3/4 Cup	4	quick
Mixed Vegetables, frozen	3 Cups	3/4 Cup	3	quick
Okra, whole medium	3 Cups	3/4 Cup	4	quick
Onions, baby pearl	3 Cups	3/4 Cup	3	quick
Onions, whole medium peeled	Half-full	1 Cup	5	quick
Parsnips, 1" cubes or slices	3 Cups	1 Cup	5	quick
Peas, in pod i.e. snow peas	3 Cups	3/4 Cup	2	quick
Peas, fresh green		NOT RECOM-MENDED		
Peas, fresh black eyes, conch, pur-ple hull, etc.	Half-full	3/4 Cup	7-8	natural
Potatoes, 1" cubes or slices, whole small new	Half-full	3/4 Cup	6-7	quick or natural
Potatoes, whole medium	3/4 full	3/4 Cup	10-11	quick or natural
Potatoes, whole large	3/4 full	1 Cup	14-15	quick or natural
Pumpkin, 2" chunks or slices	3 Cups	3/4 Cup	4-5	quick

Vegetable Cooking Time Charts

All cook times are based on a 12psi Electric Pressure Cooker. To adjust see Adapting Your Recipes in Chapter 1.

VEGETABLE	MAX QUANTITY	MIN LIQUID	MIN COOK TIME	RELEASE METHOD
Rutabaga, 1" chunks	2 Cups	3/4 Cup	6-7	quick
Spinach, fresh	3/4 full	3/4 Cup	2	quick
Spinach, frozen	3/4 full	3/4 Cup	2	quick
Squash, acorn, halved	2	1 Cup	10-11	quick
Squash, butternut, 1" cubes or slices	Half-full	3/4 Cup	5-6	quick
Squash, yellow crook neck, 1" rings	Half-full	3/4 Cup	3	quick
Squash, yellow crook neck, whole medium	3/4 full	3/4 Cup	5-6	quick
Sweet potato, peeled, 1 1/2" slices	3 Cups	3/4 Cup	7-8	quick or natural
Sweet potato, peeled, whole medium or halved large	Half-full	3/4 Cup	12-13	quick or natural
Swiss Chard	3/4 full	3/4 Cup	2	quick
Tomatoes, whole medium Plum or Roma	3/4 full	3/4 Cup	2-3	natural
Turnip, small-medium, quartered and greens	3 Cups	3/4 Cup	7-8	quick
Zucchini, 1/2" slices or chunks	3 Cups	3/4 Cup	2-3	quick

Perfect Green Beans

Prep Time: 5 minutes   Ready in: 9 minutes   Yield: 4-6 servings

INGREDIENTS
1-2 lb. fresh, whole green beans; ends trimmed
2 Tbsp butter
1 small white or yellow onion; peeled
1 Tbsp Better than Bouillon® Beef
1/2 tsp ground black pepper
3/4 Cup hot water

DIRECTIONS
1. Place your pressure cooker on a level surface, insert the pressure pot, and plug the unit in.
2. Prepare the onion by peeling it and then cutting it in half width-wise. Using the half with the root intact, score the top with a knife with an X shape; save the top half for another recipe.
3. Heat the water in a measuring cup and mix in the bouillon until dissolved.
4. Set cook time to 4 minutes (or use vegetable setting and decrease time) and press the Start button.
5. Add the butter and, when it begins to melt, place the onion into the butter, face down. Cook quickly for 1-2 minute but do not let the butter brown. Add the water/bouillon along with the pepper.
6. Toss in the green beans.
7. Attach and lock the lid of your pressure cooker.
8. Set the pressure control to "air tight" or closed.
9. When cooking time has elapsed, manually release the pressure by opening the pressure control valve to exhaust.
10. Once the pressure has been released, carefully open the lid, discard the onion and serve immediately with salt and fresh ground pepper.

TRY ADDING A CLOVE OF GARLIC OR DICED COOKED BACON
TO GIVE EVERYDAY GREEN BEANS A FLAVOR BOOST!

BRUSSELS SPROUTS

Prep Time: 5 minutes   Ready in: 16 minutes   Yield: 4-6 servings

INGREDIENTS
1 tsp olive oil
1 Cup red onion; coarsely chopped
1.25 lb. fresh Brussels sprouts; ends trimmed, brown leaves removed
1 Tbsp good balsamic vinegar
3/4 Cup chicken broth (I use 3/4 Cup of water mixed with 1 tsp better than bouillon chicken base)
1/2 tsp salt
1/2 tsp freshly-ground black pepper
Parmesan cheese (optional)

DIRECTIONS
1. Place your pressure cooker on a level surface, insert the pressure pot, and plug the unit in.
2. Press the browning feature of your pressure cooker; or set cook time to 10 minutes and press the Start button.
3. Add olive oil to the pot and when hot, add onions.
4. Sauté, stirring often, for 1-2 minutes until onion begins to soften but not turn brown.
5. Add Brussels sprouts, balsamic vinegar, chicken broth, salt and pepper to the pot; stir, close and lock the lid of your pressure cooker.
6. Set the pressure control to "air tight" or closed.
7. Press cancel to stop the browning function; set new cook time for 9 minutes and press start.
8. When cooking time has elapsed, manually release the pressure by opening the pressure control valve to exhaust.

PARSLEY POTATOES

Prep Time: 1 minutes　　　　Ready in: 15 minutes　　　　Yield: 4-6 servings

INGREDIENTS
10-15 small assorted colors fingerling potatoes or red new potatoes; washed
3 cloves garlic, peeled whole
2 tsp salt
Cool water to cover
1 stick butter; divided

DIRECTIONS
1. Place your pressure cooker on a level surface, insert the pressure pot, and plug the unit in.
2. Add 1/2 stick of butter, garlic and 2 tsp salt.
3. Add just enough water to cover the potatoes.
4. Attach and lock the lid of your pressure cooker; set the pressure control to "air tight" or closed.
5. Set cook time to 10 minutes and press the Start button.
6. When cooking time has elapsed, manually release the pressure by opening the pressure control valve to exhaust.
7. Once the pressure has been released, carefully open the lid.
8. Drain the potatoes. Place cooked potatoes back into the pressure pan along with the other 1/2 stick of butter and the chopped parsley. Keep on Keep Warm for up to 15 minutes before gently tossing and serving. .

Buttery Corn-on-the-Cob

Prep Time: 5-10 minutes   Ready in: 12 minutes   Yield: 4-6 servings

INGREDIENTS
4-12 ears of fresh corn; husk and silk removed
1 stick of butter
1/3 C water
2 tsp salt
1/4 tsp granulated sugar

DIRECTIONS
1. Place your pressure cooker on a level surface, insert the pressure pot, and plug the unit in.
2. If you have a low rack or trivet, use it. Add all ingredients.
3. Attach and lock the lid of your pressure cooker; set the pressure control to "air tight" or closed.
4. Set cook time to 7 minutes and press the Start button.
5. When cooking time has elapsed, manually release the pressure by opening the pressure control valve to exhaust.
6. Once the pressure has been released, carefully open the lid and stir.
7. Use tongs to transfer corn to a platter, ladle butter sauce over corn and serve immediately.

TV Tidbit - when cooking corn on the cob on TV we often stack the corn on end so that we can show a larger capacity. Although you can cook the corn this way, I suggest you use 2 Cups of water, brought to an almost-boil before putting in the corn. This will prevent the corn from burning on the bottom.

AGAVE CARROTS

Prep Time: 5 minutes   Ready in: 12 minutes   Yield: 4-6 servings

INGREDIENTS

1 lb. baby carrots (not snack size)
1 Tbsp butter
1/2 Cup water
2 tsp agave light syrup
1 tsp orange zest
2 tsp fresh parsley (optional)

DIRECTIONS

1. Place your pressure cooker on a level surface, insert the pressure pot, and plug the unit in.
2. Add all ingredients except for the parsley; stir.
3. Attach and lock the lid of your pressure cooker; set the pressure control to "air tight" or closed.
4. Set cook time to 7 minutes and press the Start button.
5. When cooking time has elapsed, manually release the pressure by opening the pressure control valve to exhaust.
6. Once the pressure has been released, carefully open the lid and stir.
7. Sprinkle the fresh parsley over the carrots and serve immediately.

ARTICHOKES
Prep Time: 10 minutes   Ready in: 18 minutes   Yield: 4 servings or 12-15 appetizer servings.

INGREDIENTS
4 large artichokes; stem trimmed and leaf-tips snipped
1 stick of butter; cut into pieces
2 cloves garlic; peeled and thinly sliced
1/4 C water
1/4 C dry white wine
Zest from 1 lemon
1 lemon; halved, juiced

DIRECTIONS
1. Trim the bottom of the artichokes so that they will stand up.
2. Using kitchen shears, snip off the ends of the leaves as shown in photo below. Tuck pieces of butter and slices of garlic randomly throughout the leaves of all artichokes.
3. Place your pressure cooker on a level surface, insert the pressure pot, and plug the unit in.
4. Place the artichokes into the bottom of the pressure cooker (or into a steamer basket). Mix the liquids together with the zest and pour over all.
5. Attach and lock the lid of your pressure cooker; set the pressure control to "air tight" or closed.
6. Set cook time to 15 minutes and press the Start button.
7. When cooking time has elapsed, manually release the pressure by opening the pressure control valve to exhaust.
8. Once the pressure has been released, carefully open the lid.
9. Use tongs to transfer artichokes to individual dishes or on one large platter. Ladle the sauce from the pan over top
10. Serve hot with a cold Dip made from 1/4 C Mayo mixed with 1 tsp lemon juice and 1/4 tsp garlic salt.

TV Tidbit - Whenever we cook artichokes on HSN, everyone scrambles after the show to grab a doggie bag! I always try to get at least two and since this demo is done in a 10 qt pressure cooker, there are PLENTY to go around!

Red Cabbage Kraut

Prep Time: 15 minutes   Ready in: 20 minutes   Yield: 10-12 servings

INGREDIENTS
6 slices bacon; coarsely chopped
1 large onion; chopped fine
1 very large red cabbage; shredded
1 Tbs + 2 tsp salt
1 Tbs ground black pepper
2 bay leaves
½ cup white vinegar
1 apple; cored, and chopped
½ cup water

DIRECTIONS
1. Place your pressure cooker on a level surface, insert the pressure pot, and plug the unit in.
2. Set cook time to 10 minutes and press Start.
3. When the pan is hot add the bacon; stir quickly and cook until beginning to brown.
4. Add the onion and cook another 3-4 minutes or until the onion begins to soften but is not browned.
5. Add the remaining ingredients and stir gently to mix.
6. Attach and lock the lid of your pressure cooker; set the pressure control to "air tight" or closed.
7. Press the Cancel button and reset the cook time for 10 minutes; press Start.
8. When cooking is complete, cancel the keep warm feature and let rest 5 minutes before manually exhausting the pressure.
9. Once the pressure has been released, carefully open the lid and stir well.

Swiss Chard with Warm Bacon Vinaigrette

Prep Time: 15 minutes   Ready in: 20 minutes   Yield: 6-8 servings

INGREDIENTS
4 slices bacon; cooked and coarsely chopped
1 medium red onion; cut in strips
24 Cups Swiss chard, chopped (about 20 ounces)
1 Tbs + 2 tsp salt
1 Tbs ground black pepper
1 Tbsp cider vinegar
3/4 cup water

DIRECTIONS
1. Place your pressure cooker on a level surface, insert the pressure pot, and plug the unit in.
2. Set cook time to 3 minutes and press Start.
3. When the pan is hot add the bacon; stir quickly and cook until crispy; drain on paper towel and chop.
4. Add the onion and cook another 3-4 minutes or until the onion begins to soften.
5. Add the water and scrape the bottom of the pan. Add the salt and pepper. Add the Swiss chard to the top of the water, do not stir.
6. Attach and lock the lid of your pressure cooker; set the pressure control to "air tight" or closed.
7. When cooking is complete, cancel the keep warm feature and let rest 5 minutes before manually exhausting the pressure.
8. Once the pressure has been released, carefully open the lid and stir well. Stir in the vinegar.
9. Drain before serving and top with the chopped bacon

CAULIFLOWER

Prep Time: 15 minutes   Ready in: 25 minutes   Yield: 6-8 servings

INGREDIENTS
1 head cauliflower
1 Tbs + 2 tsp salt
1 Tbs ground black pepper
3/4 cup water
2-3 Tbsp butter

DIRECTIONS
1. Prepare the cauliflower by trimming off any green leaves, excessive stem and brown spots.
1. Place your pressure cooker on a level surface, insert the pressure pot, and plug the unit in.
2. Set cook time to 8 minutes and press Start.
3. Add water to the bottom of the pot along with 1 Tbsp salt.
4. Place a rack into the cooker and sit the cauliflower on te rack.
5. Attach and lock the lid of your pressure cooker; set the pressure control to "air tight" or closed.
6. When cooking is complete, cancel the keep warm feature and immediately exhaust the pressure.
7. Once the pressure has been released, carefully open the lid .
8. Lay the pats of butter on the cauliflower along ith the shredded cheese. Replace lid, keeping the pressure valve in the Exhaust position.
9. Wait 2-3 minutes, or until the cheese is melting, and transfer the cauliflower to a serving dish.
10. Serve hot with salt and pepper.

Sweet Potato Mash

Prep Time: 5 minutes   Ready in: 30 minutes   Yield: 4-6 servings

INGREDIENTS

3-4 large sweet potatoes; peeled and halved
4 Tbsp butter
3 tsp salt
4 Cups water
1 Cup orange juice
1/4 tsp cinnamon
1/8 tsp nutmeg
1/4 Cup warm milk
Chopped pecans (optional)

DIRECTIONS

1. Place your pressure cooker on a level surface, insert the pressure pot, and plug the unit in.
2. Add halved potatoes and 2 Tbsp butter.
3. Add 4 Cups of water and 1 Cup orange juice. This should almost cover the potatoes; add water if needed.
4. Attach and lock the lid of your pressure cooker; set the pressure control to "air tight" or closed.
5. Press the preprogrammed Yams/Potato button or set cook time to 13 minutes; press Start.
6. When cooking time has elapsed, manually release the pressure and carefully open the lid.
7. Drain the potatoes saving 1 Cup of the liquid. Place cooked potatoes into a medium mixing bowl and add the remaining butter along with the salt, cinnamon, nutmeg.
8. Using the medium speed of your hand mixer, whip to desired consistency slowly adding the hot liquid from the potatoes. If needed, add the milk as well.
9. Serve immediately with butter and toasted pecans if desired.

MAKES A GREAT HOLIDAY TAKE-ALONG SIDE DISH!
SIMPLY SPREAD POTATOES INTO A BUTTERED CASSEROLE DISH, TOP WITH PECANS OR MARSHMALLOWS
AND BAKE FOR 10 MINUTES IN A 375 OVEN!

CHEESY GARLIC SMASHED POTATOES

Prep Time: 1 minutes   Ready in: 12 minutes   Yield: 4-6 servings

INGREDIENTS
10 med white potatoes, halved; peel 7 (or all if preferred)
3 cloves garlic, peeled whole
3 tsp salt
cool water to cover
1 tsp coarse ground black pepper
½ stick butter, melted
¾ Cup half-and-half, warmed
1 Cup shredded sharp cheddar

DIRECTIONS
1. Place your pressure cooker on a level surface, insert the pressure pot, and plug the unit in.
2. Add halved potatoes, garlic and 2 tsp salt.
3. Add just enough water to cover the potatoes.
4. Attach and lock the lid of your pressure cooker; set the pressure control to "air tight" or closed.
5. Set cook time to 10 minutes and press the Start button.
6. When cooking time has elapsed, manually release the pressure by opening the pressure control valve to exhaust.
7. Once the pressure has been released, carefully open the lid.
8. Drain the potatoes. Place cooked potatoes into a medium mixing bowl and add the remaining salt, pepper, butter and half-and-half.
9. Using the medium speed of your hand mixer, whip to desired consistency adding more half-and-half if needed. Add cheese and mix in on lowest speed.
10. Adjust salt and pepper to taste and serve immediately.

MAKES A GREAT TAKE-ALONG SIDE DISH!
SIMPLY SPREAD POTATOES INTO A BUTTERED CASSEROLE DISH, TOP WITH EXTRA CHEESE
AND BAKE FOR 10 MINUTES IN A 375 OVEN!

ASPARAGUS

Prep Time: 15 minutes   Ready in: 15 minutes   Yield: 6-8 servings

INGREDIENTS
2 Tbsp butter
2 cloves garlic; minced
1 tsp salt
1 Tbs ground black pepper
1 lb asparagus; thin to medium stalks
3/4 cup water

DIRECTIONS
1. Prepare the asparagus by trimming off the woody end where they naturally break when bending the stalk.
1. Place your pressure cooker on a level surface, insert the pressure pot, and plug the unit in.
2. Set cook time to 3 minutes and press Start.
3. Add butter to the pot along with the garlic, salt and pepper.
4. Place the asparagus directly in the pan and toss in the butter. Pour the water over the asparagus.
5. Attach and lock the lid of your pressure cooker; set the pressure control to "air tight" or closed.
6. When cooking is complete, cancel the keep warm feature and immediately exhaust the pressure.
7. Once the pressure has been released, carefully open the lid .
8. Use tongs and serve immediately!

CRANBERRY STUFFING

Prep Time: 10 minutes   Ready in: 30 minutes   Yield: 4-6 servings

INGREDIENTS
1/4 - 3/4 Cups cranberries; whole
1 1/2 Cup chicken broth
4 Tbsp butter
1/2 Cup onion; minced
1/2 Cup celery; minced
1/4 Cup fresh parsley; chopped
12 oz package Pepperidge Farm® Cubed herb seasoned stuffing

DIRECTIONS
1. Place your pressure cooker on a level surface, insert the pressure pot, and plug the unit in.
2. Add the butter, onion, celery, parsley and 1 1/2 Cups chicken broth.
3. When the liquid begins to boil add in the stuffing cubes and cranberries. Quickly toss to moisten.
4. Immediately attach and lock the lid of your pressure cooker; set the pressure control to "air tight" or closed.
5. Press the preprogrammed seafood button or set cook time to 3 minutes; press Start.
6. When cooking time has elapsed, immediately release the pressure. Carefully open the lid.
7. Use as stuffing for a turkey or chicken, serve immediately as-is or spoon into a baking dish and brown in the oven.

GET AN OVEN-BAKED STYLE OF STUFFING BY PLACING THE STUFFING INTO A BUTTERED CASSEROLE
DISH AND BAKING FOR 10 MINUTES IN A 400 OVEN!

Note: the cranberries tend to make the stuffing a bit tart so do not use more than
3/4 Cup. Reduce to 1/4 Cup your first time and adjust from there!

About Cooking Meat & Poultry

A common misconception about pressure cooking is because the meat is cooking in a moist, airtight environment, it cannot be overcooked. Wrong!

Because of the high heats under pressure, the fibers in the meat shrink both in length and width, thus squeezing the moisture out. Even though the meat is covered with liquid, it can still be dry.

IT IS VERY IMPORTANT THAT YOU CONSULT THE COOK TIME CHARTS AND USE YOUR INTUITIVENESS WHERE DIFFERENT MEATS ARE CONCERNED.

It's the little things that make the difference!
- Make sure meat is cut into uniform pieces for even cooking.
- Brown meat and poultry on all sides before pressure cooking to enhance the flavor and appearance. Refer to the Browning & Searing section for complete instructions.
- Remove the skin from chicken parts before pressure cooking makes for a more attractive and lower fat finished dish.
- Use a variety of flavorful liquids such as wine, condensed soup, diluted marinades, double-strength broth. The flavor of the liquid will be infused into the meat so why use plain water?
- Fattier cuts of meat will yield a tastier result. However, to avoid a greasy meal, cook the meat 3/4 of the way, drain, replace with fresh liquid and continue cooking until tender.
- Unless otherwise noted, release pressure using the Cold Water or Natural Release Method.

ALL VARIETIES OF MEATS - COOKING TIME CHARTS - NEXT 4 PAGES

Meat Lovers Meals

If you use your pressure cooker for only one thing...use it for large cuts of meat!

Ribs, Roasts and whole Chickens all cook deliciously in a fraction of the time and yield that fall-off-the-bone tenderness meat-lovers crave!

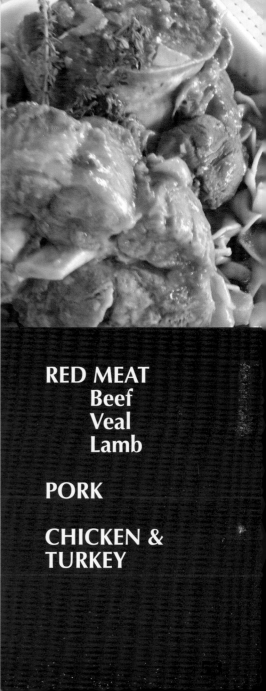

RED MEAT
Beef
Veal
Lamb

PORK

CHICKEN & TURKEY

Cooking Time Charts for Meats

MEAT VARIETY	BROWN?	MINIMUM LIQUID	MIN COOK TIME	RELEASE METHOD
BEEF & RED MEAT				
Beef Brisket, fresh or corned; 3-4 lb	no	2 Cups	50-75 min	Natural
Beef Cubes or Stew Meat; 1 - 1 1/2" ; up to 3 lb	yes	1 Cup	15-20 min	Natural
Beef Heart; 3-4 lb	no	cover	50-75 min	Natural
Beef Kidney	no	cover	8-10 min	Natural
Beef Liver; sliced	yes	1 Cup	5 min	Natural
Beef Meatballs; 1-2 lb	yes	1 Cup	10-12 min	Natural
Beef Meatloaf; 2-3 lb	no	1 Cup	15-20 min	Natural
Beef Oxtails	yes	cover	40-45 min	Natural
Beef Pot Roast, rib, round, rump, chuck, blade; 3-4 lb.	yes	2 Cups	50-60 min	Natural
Beef Shank; 1 1/2- 2 1/2" thick	yes	1 1/2 Cups	35-45 min	Natural
Beef Short Ribs; 3-4 lb.	yes	1 1/2 Cups	30-40 min	Natural
Beef Steak, rump, round, chuck or blade; 1-2" thick; up to 3 lb	yes	1 Cup	20-25 min	Natural
Beef Tongue, fresh or smoked; 2-3 lb.	no	cover	75-90 min	Natural
Beef Tripe honeycomb; 2 lb	no	cover	40-45 min	Natural
Goat, young			Cook as for similar cuts of Lamb	
Goat, mature			Cook as for similar cuts of Venison	
Lamb Chops, 1/2" thick	yes	3/4 Cup	5 min	Quick
Lamb Chops, 1" thick	yes	3/4 Cup	9 min	Quick

Cooking Time Charts for Meats

MEAT VARIETY	BROWN?	MINIMUM LIQUID	MIN COOK TIME	RELEASE METHOD
Lamb Leg, 3 lb.	yes	1 1/2 Cups	20-25 min	Natural
Lamb Shoulder Roast, bone-in, 3-5 lb.	yes	2 Cups	25-35 min	Natural
Lamb Stew Meat, 1" cubes	yes	1 Cup	12-15 min	Natural
Veal Chops up to 1" thick	yes	3/4 Cup	5-7 min	Quick
Veal Shanks, up to 3" thick	yes	1 Cup	25-35 min	Natural
Veal Stew Meat, 1" cubes, up to 2 lb.	yes	2 Cups	10-12 min	Natural
Venison Roast, any cut, 3-4" thick	yes	2 Cups	40-45 min	Natural
Venison, cubed, thin sliced, steaks or chops up to 1" thick	yes	3/4 Cup	20-25 min	Natural
Venison, Ground Meat	yes	3/4 Cup	12-15 min	Natural
PORK				
Pork, Ham Hocks, smoked	no	cover	45 min	Natural
Pork, Ham Picnic or Shoulder (fresh,uncooked), 3-5 lb	no	2 1/2 Cups	40-50 min	Natural
Pork, Ham Shank or Butt (fresh, uncooked), 3-5 lb.	no	2 1/2 Cups	50-60 min	Natural
Pork Chops or Steaks, up to 1" thick	yes	3/4 Cup	6 min	Natural
Pork Chops or Steaks, over 1" thick or stuffed	yes	3/4 Cup	8-10 min	Natural
Pork Loin Roast, 3-4 lb	yes	1 Cup	25-35 min	Natural
Pork, Pigs feet	no	cover	45 min	Natural
Pork Ribs, spareribs, baby back, bone-in, single rack, up to 4 lb, grill-able	no	3/4 Cup	40 min	Natural

Cooking Time Charts for Meats

MEAT VARIETY	BROWN?	MINIMUM LIQUID	MIN COOK TIME	RELEASE METHOD
Pork Ribs, spareribs, baby back, bone-in, single rack, up to 4 lb, fall-or-the-bone	no	1 Cup	55 min	Natural
Pork Shoulder, Arm or Blade Roast, bone-in or boneless, 3-4 lb., shred-able	yes	2 Cups	45-50 min	Natural
Pork Sausage, Italian, Polish, Kielbasa, steam on rack	yes	3/4 Cup	8 min	Quick
Pork Stew Meat, 1 1/2" cubes	yes	3/4 Cup	10-12 min	Natural
CHICKEN & POULTRY				
Chicken Breast; bone-in, up to 3 lb of .30 lb individual pieces	yes	1 Cup	7 min	Natural
Chicken Breast; boneless, up to 3 lb of .30 lb individual pieces	yes	1 Cup	6 min	Natural
Chicken Breast; boneless strips, tenders	yes	1/2 Cup	4 min	Quick
Chicken Livers	no	1 Cup	3 min	Quick
Chicken, Ground Meat	yes	3/4 Cup	4 min	Quick
Chicken, legs or thighs, bone-in, up to 3 lb	yes	3/4 Cup	7 min	Quick
Chicken, legs or thighs, boneless, up to 3 lb	yes	3/4 Cup	6 min	Quick
Chicken Sausage, Italian, Polish, Kielbasa, steam on rack	yes	3/4 Cup	8 min	Quick
Chicken Wings	no	3/4 Cup	6 min	Quick

Cooking Time Charts for Meats

MEAT VARIETY	BROWN?	MINIMUM LIQUID	MIN COOK TIME	RELEASE METHOD
Chicken, Whole 2 - 3 lb. (not stuffed)	no	1 Cup	18-20 min	Natural
Chicken, Whole 3 - 4 lb. (not stuffed)	no	1 Cup	20-25 min	Natural
Cornish Hen, whole	no	3/4 Cup	8-10 min	Natural
Duck, cut into pieces	yes	3/4 Cup; use rack	8-10 min	Natural
Duck, whole, 3- 4 lb.	yes	1 Cup; use rack	25-30 min	Natural
Turkey Breast, boneless, 3 lb.	no	1 Cup	20-22 min	Natural
Turkey Breast, bone-in, 3-4 lb.	no	1 Cup	20-25 min	Natural
Turkey Breast, ground meat	no	3/4 Cup	8-10 min	Natural
Turkey Legs, up to 6	yes	3/4 Cup	12 min	Natural
Turkey Sausage, Italian, Polish, Kielbasa, steam on rack	yes	3/4 Cup	8 min	Natural

Meatloaf Minis

Prep Time: 15 minutes   Ready in: 1 hour   Yield: each loaf serves 2

INGREDIENTS
2 1/4 lb. ground extra lean beef
1 large egg; beaten
1 small onion; minced (about 1/2 Cup)
1/2 small red or green bell pepper; minced (about 1/2 Cup)
2 tsp dried parsley flakes or 2 Tbsp fresh chopped parsley
1 tsp dried thyme leaves or 1 Tbsp fresh thyme
1/2 cup Progressive seasoned bread crumbs
1/2 Cup mozzarella cheese; shredded
2 Tbsp plus 3 Tbsp tomato paste
3/4 Cup water mixed with 1 Tbsp tomato paste
1/2 cup mozzarella cheese; shredded.

DIRECTIONS
1. Prepare the meatloaves by beating the egg in the bottom of a large mixing bowl. Add in 2 Tbsp of the tomato paste followed by the onion, pepper and garlic, parsley, basil and bread crumbs. Mix in the meat followed by 1/2 Cup of the mozzarella cheese. Use your hands to blend as evenly as possible.
2. Divide the meat in half and make 2 loaves.
1. Place pressure cooker on a level surface, insert the pot and plug in. Set pressure cooking time to 25 minutes; press Start.
2. Whisk the 1 Tbsp of tomato paste into the 3/4 Cup water; pour into the pressure cooker.
3. Place the meatloaves into the pot.
4. Secure the lid, turn pressure valve to Air Tight.
5. When the cooking time has elapsed turn the keep warm feature off and let pressure release naturally.
6. While the pressure is releasing, preheat the low broiler in your oven.
7. When the pressure has released , carefully open the lid.
8. Use tongs and a spatula to carefully move meat loaves from the pot to a cookie sheet. Spread the top of each meatloaf with 2 Tbs Tomato paste and shredded cheese.
9. Place the cookie sheet with the meatloaves into the oven on a low-center rack.
10. Broil until tomato and cheese is hot and bubbly. Serve with mashed or scalloped potatoes.

CORNED BEEF

Prep Time: 15 minutes   Ready in: 70 minutes   Yield: 1 serving per 1/3 pound meat

INGREDIENTS
1 corned beef with seasoning packet; 3-7 lb.
1 tsp onion salt
1 tsp celery salt
1 Tbsp coarse ground mustard
1 Tbsp brown sugar
1 bottle of beer; darker is better (but it's up to you!)
6-15 small red potatoes
1/2 lb. peeled baby carrots or 1-inch rings of large carrots
1 small-medium head cabbage

DIRECTIONS
1. Prepare the meat by removing the corned beef from the package and rinsing off the surface brine. Lay the corned beef onto a cutting board and sprinkle the onion salt, celery salt, brown sugar and mustard over the meat. Use your hands and massage the seasonings into the meat.
2. Looking at the pot of your pressure cooker, decide if the meat must be cut down to fit inside. Ideally you will leave the meat whole and either stand it on end "curling" it along the inside edge (fat side out) or just laying it inside the pot flat or arched (fat side up). However, if it is just too large, cut the meat in half or however is necessary to fit!
3. When the meat is in the pan, sprinkle in the seasoning packet and add the bottle of beer. Fill the pot with cool water until the meat is submerged by 1 inch.
4. Plug in the pressure cooker, secure the lid and set pressure valve Air Tight.
5. Set the Cook Time for 1 hour and 15 minutes. Press Start.
6. While the meat is cooking, prepare the veggies by washing and peeling the potatoes (if desired), washing, peeling and cutting large carrots into 1-inch rings or just washing the pre-peeled baby carrots. For the cabbage, pull off and discard any spotted or wilted outer leaves and the cut the cabbage in half lengthwise. Use a sharp knife and cut a "V" shape removing the hard core from the end and extending up into the cabbage.   Chop the desired amount of cabbage into large bite-size pieces; do not shred or finely chop! Place all the veggies into a bowl, cover with a wet paper towel and place into the fridge.
7. When cooking time has elapsed, turn the pressure cooker off. Let sit 10 minutes and then release the remaining pressure. Carefully open the lid and remove the meat to a cutting board. Let the liquid remain

untouched in the pot.

8. When cool enough to handle, use a sharp knife and slice away the majority of the fat on the meat; discard.

9. Using a measuring cup or turkey baster, carefully remove as much fatty oil from the top of the liquid as you can. You want to leave a small amount of fat to season the vegetables so do not use a separator.

10. Reload the pot first with the potatoes and carrots, then with the meat and top with the cabbage. If you find that you now have too much liquid, use a measuring cup and remove however much you need to have a 4-inch space at the top of the pot.

11. Replace the lid, set the valve to Air Tight and set the cook time to 15 minutes; press Start.

12. When the time has elapsed, turn the pressure cooker off and let the pressure release naturally.

13. Carefully open the lid and remove the meat to a cutting board.

14. To serve, slice the meat, against the grain, and serve with the vegetables and a side of stone ground mustard or prepared horseradish.

SUNDAY ROAST

Prep Time: 15 minutes   Ready in: 70 minutes   Yield: 1 serving per 1/3 pound meat

INGREDIENTS
3-4 lb. Round Roast
2 Tbsp vegetable oil
1 Tbsp Balsamic vinegar
½ Cup good red wine
1 clove garlic; minced
1 med onion; coarsely chopped
1 Tbsp Worcestershire sauce
1 Tbsp ketchup
1 Tbsp Better Than Bouillon beef bouillon base
1 tsp salt
1 tsp coarse ground black pepper
1 tsp fresh rosemary; chopped plus additional for garnish
1 1/2 Cup hot water
8-10 small fingerling potatoes
8-10 baby carrots
To Make Gravy
3 Tbsp butter
2 Tbsp flour
3 Cups strained stock
3 Tbsp cream or whole milk

DIRECTIONS
1. Place your pressure cooker on a level surface, insert the pressure pot, and plug the unit in.
2. Set Cook Time for 10 minutes or select the preprogrammed Brown Button. Press Start.
3. Add the oil and, when hot, use long tongs to brown roast; about 1-2 minutes on each side (and end) until it is golden brown. Remove roast to platter and set aside.
4. Add vinegar and wine and scrape bottom with spatula. Add onion and garlic, sauté 1 minute.   Add next the next 6 ingredients. Stir in the water and place roast back in pan scattering the fingerling potatoes and carrots around roast, if desired.
5. Attach lid and set the pressure valve to Air Tight (closed). Press Cancel and then set the cook time for 50

minutes. Press Start.

6. When the cooking time has elapsed, press the Cancel button to turn off the Keep Warm feature.

7. Manually release the pressure, remove lid and place roast on platter to rest.

8. Carefully remove the pressure pot and strain the liquid, through a sieve, over a bowl or large measuring cup. Reserve 3 cups.

To make to gravy:

• Press the Brown button on the pressure cooker or set cook time to 10 minutes; press Start.

• Add butter and allow to melt. Sprinkle in flour and mix to a paste.

• Slowly add reserved liquid, stirring constantly, once the mixture begins to boil, turn the pressure cooker to Keep Warm.

• Simmer until thickened and then stir in cream or milk.

To serve:

Slice roast and serve with gravy over all or on the side. Serve with the veggies.

Beef Bourguignon

Prep: 15 min   Ready in: 70 min   Yield: 6-8 servings

INGREDIENTS
2 lb. beef Chuck Roast, cut in 1" cubes
1 Tbsp vegetable oil
4 slices bacon; cut ½" pieces
1 med onion; diced
3 cloves garlic; crushed
½ tsp salt
¼ tsp ground thyme
1 Tbsp dried parsley
1 ½ bay leaves
1/4 tsp ground pepper
1 Cup burgundy wine, reserve ¼ cup
1/2 Cup water
4 Tbsp flour
15 pearl onions
15 baby Bella or Button mushrooms
8 oz egg noodles; cooked Al dente.

DIRECTIONS
1. Place your pressure cooker on a level surface, insert the pressure pot, and plug the unit in.
2. Set Cook Time for 10 minutes or select the preprogrammed Brown Button. Press Start.
3. Add the oil and, when hot, add the bacon and onion and cook 2-3 minutes or until bacon is beginning to brown. Add the beef and cook another 3 minutes, stirring constantly.   Add the garlic and other herbs along with the wine and water.
4. Attach and lock lid. Set the pressure valve to Air Tight (closed). Press Cancel and set cook time to 40 minutes (or press preprogrammed soup/stew button) and press Start. When the cooking time has elapsed, release pressure and remove lid. Make a slurry by mixing the reserved ¼ cup wine with the flour.   Stir the wine slurry into the pot and add the pearl onions and mushrooms.   Replace lid, close valve and set timer for 4 minutes. When the cooking time has elapsed, let pressure drop naturally.
5. While waiting for the pressure to drop, cook the egg noodles in boiling water as directed on package; drain noodles. Serve the beef, gravy and mushrooms over a bed of noodles. Offer salt and pepper for extra seasoning.

BARBECUE BRISKET

Prep Time: 10 minutes - plus 8 hours marinade time   Ready in: 1 hour 40 minutes   Yield: allow 1/4 lb. per serving

INGREDIENTS
4-6 lb. Beef Brisket; trimmed of fat
½ tsp garlic salt
½ tsp onion salt
½ tsp celery salt
1 4-oz. Bottle Liquid Smoke; save 3 teaspoons for the sauce
Sauce:
2 Cups ketchup
½ Cup vinegar
½ Cup sugar
¼ tsp garlic salt
¼ tsp onion salt
¼ tsp celery salt
3 tsp Liquid Smoke
½ Cup Worcestershire sauce

DIRECTIONS
1. Wash and pat dry the brisket. Place it into an airtight container or onto a metal baking pan that can be covered with plastic wrap. Sprinkle with the seasonings and coat all over with the Liquid Smoke. Cover and refrigerate at least 8 hours.
2. Remove the brisket from the refrigerator and pour off any remaining marinade.
3. Place the pressure cooker on a level surface, insert the pot and plug in.
4. Set Cook Time for 90 minutes. Press Start.
5. Add all of the Sauce ingredients above and bring to a low boil, stirring often. Let simmer for 3-4 minutes.
6. Place the brisket into the sauce; you may have to cut the brisket into 2 pieces if it won't fit into the pot.
7. Secure the lid and set the pressure valve to Air Tight.
8. When the cooking time has elapsed, unplug the pressure cooker and let the pressure release naturally until you can safely remove the lid.
9. Remove the brisket to a cutting board and slice thinly against the grain. Serve immediately or return the slices to the pot with the sauce.

Beef Baby Back Ribs

Prep Time: 5 minutes   Ready in: 1 hour 40 minutes

INGREDIENTS
1 Tbsp honey
1/4 Cup paprika
1/2 Tbsp salt
1 Tbsp cayenne pepper
1 Tbsp garlic powder
1 Tbsp onion powder
1 can ginger ale
2 lb. beef or pork back or loin ribs
½ Cup BBQ sauce; homemade or your favorite brand

DIRECTIONS
1. Wash the ribs and pat dry. Rub the meaty side of each rack with 1/2 Tbsp honey. Mix the spices together in a small bowl and then sprinkle liberally over both racks.
2. Plug in the pressure cooker and place the pot insert inside. Add the ginger ale to the pot.
3. Put the ribs into the cooker by either cutting the rack in half or thirds and laying them down into the pot (recommended if you are planning on crisping them on the grill) or stand them on end by wrapping the first rack around the inside of the pot in a spiral and then spiraling the next rack inside of the first, and so on (recommended if you are cooking more than 2 racks). Pour or baste the BBQ sauce directly onto the ribs.
4. Secure the lid and close the pressure valve to Air Tight.
5. To prepare these for the grill, set Cook Time to 60 minutes.
6. For "fall-off-the-bone" ribs straight from the pressure cooker, set the Cook Time for 80 minutes.
7. After the cooking time has elapsed, unplug (or turn off) the pressure cooker. The pressure may be released immediately by opening the valve or naturally by waiting until the pressure has dissipated and the lid can safely be removed.
8. Carefully remove ribs from pot and serve immediately with BBQ sauce or place on a hot grill or under the broiler for 5 minutes per side for that crispy, char-grill taste.

TV Tidbit - Ribs made the Elite brand pressure cooker famous on HSN! It's hard to watch the bones easily pulling away from the moist, tender meat without your mouth watering. Then when you see the full 2-3 racks that come out of the cooker...Well let's just say that many owners of the Elite PC will agree that the ribs prompted their purchase of an Electric PC!

Osso Bucco

Prep Time: 15 minutes   Ready in: 60 minutes   Yield: 1 serving per 1/3 pound meat

INGREDIENTS

1/2 Cup flour
1 tsp salt
1 tsp paprika
3-4 lb. Veal shanks (2-3" thick)
½ Cup olive oil
½ Cup carrots; chopped
1/3 Cup onion; chopped
½ red pepper; seeds and membrane removed, meat chopped
2 cloves garlic; chopped
¾ Cup white wine (I use Sauvignon Blanc)
3 sprigs Thyme
3-4 small celery stalks with leaves attached
2 Cups hot water
1 ½ Tbsp Better Than Bouillon Beef flavor stock
1 15-ounce can of tomato sauce
2 bay leaves
4 Cups wide egg noodles - cooked to desired texture

DIRECTIONS

1. Ready the ingredients by placing the flour, salt and paprika into a zip-top baggie and pre-chopping the onion, carrots, peppers and garlic.

2. Plug in the pressure cooker, select the preprogrammed Brown button or set Cook Time to 10 minutes; press Start. Add the olive oil to the pan. Place the veal shanks into the baggie of flour and shake to coat well. When the oil is hot, use tongs and lower the shanks into the pot. Brown 2-3 minutes on each side and then remove to a plate.

3. Add the onion, carrot and peppers to the pot and sauté for about 1 minute. Add the garlic, stir well and then add the wine. Bring to a boil. Add the thyme and the celery stalks and let the mixture cook for 2-3 minutes.

4. Stir in the water, beef bouillon, tomato sauce and bay leaves. Use the tongs to lower each shank into the liquid, turning over a couple of times to coat with the liquid. Secure the lid and set the pressure valve to Air Tight. Press Cancel, set the cooking time for 45 minutes and press Start. When the cooking time has elapsed, press the Start/Stop button to cancel the Keep Warm function. Release the pressure manually, open lid and stir. Serve with the egg noodles and offer the extra sauce on the side.

ALL AMERICAN POT ROAST WITH VEGGIES
Prep Time: 15 min   Ready in: 80 min   Yield: 1/3 lb meat per serving

INGREDIENTS
3-4 lb. Round Roast
2 Tbsp vegetable oil
½ Cup good red wine
1 clove garlic; minced
1 medium onion; coarsely chopped
1 Tbsp Worcestershire sauce
1 Tbsp ketchup
1 Tbsp Better Than Bouillon beef bouillon base
1 tsp salt
1 tsp coarse ground black pepper
1 tsp celery salt
hot water
½ lb. Baby carrots
10-12 small red potatoes
4 celery ribs; cut into 1" pieces
1 Tbsp cornstarch
1 Cup cold water

DIRECTIONS
1. Place your pressure cooker on a level surface, insert the pressure pot, and plug the unit in.
2. Set Cook Time for 10 minutes or select the preprogrammed Brown Button. Press Start.
3. Add the oil and, when hot, sear the roast; about 1 minute on each side and end. Remove roast and set aside.
4. Add the wine and scrape bottom of the pan with spatula. Add onion and garlic, sauté 1 minute. Add next the next 6 ingredients, stir. Place roast back in pan and just cover with hot water. Attach lid and set the pressure valve to Air Tight (closed).
5. Set timer for 50 minutes and press Start. When the cooking time has elapsed, release pressure, remove lid and add vegetables. Replace lid, set valve to Air Tight and set the timer for 15 minutes. Release pressure slowly, remove lid and stir gently. Press Cancel and then set the cook time for 3 minutes. Meanwhile, in a small bowl or cup mix cornstarch and water together. When the pot roast begins to boil, pour into liquid around roast.
6. Set the Pressure Cooker to Keep Warm and simmer slowly until gravy thickens. Serve within the hour with plenty of bread or rolls. Or have them as Hoagies (pictured above).

SPANISH BEEF

Prep Time: 10 minutes   Ready in: 50 minutes   Yield: 6-8 servings

INGREDIENTS
2 lb. sirloin steak; cut into single-serving sized pieces
½ Cup flour
1 tsp salt
1 tsp pepper
2 Tbsp olive oil
2 Tbsp butter
1 large Spanish onion; cut into thin rings.
1/4 Cup diced Chorizo
2 cloves garlic
¼ Cup dry red cooking wine
2 14.5 cans diced tomatoes
¼ Cup beef broth
1 bay leaf
½ tsp thyme
1/2 Cup pimento-stuffed Spanish green olives; small
3 Cups white rice; cooked according to package directions

DIRECTIONS
1. Place the steak into a baggie with the flour, 1/2 tsp salt and 1/2 tsp pepper and toss to coat.
2. Place the pressure cooker on a level surface, insert the pot and plug in.
3. Press the preprogrammed Brown button or set Cook Time for 5 minutes; press Start. Add the olive oil.
4. When the oil is hot, carefully add the breaded meat to the oil (work in small batches to avoid overcrowding in the pan) and fry 1-2 minutes on each side or until lightly browned.
5. Remove meat and drain on paper towels. Repeat process until all the meat is cooked; add more oil as needed.
6. While the meat drains, add the diced onion, garlic and Chorizo to the pan. Sauté for 1-2 minutes or until hot a sizzling. Add wine, tomatoes, beef broth, bay leaf and thyme. Add the steak back to the mixture.
7. Secure lid onto the pressure cooker, set pressure valve to Air Tight. Press the preprogrammed Beef button or set Cook Time to 30 minutes.
8. After the 30 minutes is up, quickly release the pressure and remove the lid. Use tongs to turn the steaks over and stir the mixture. Add the olives.
9. Reposition the lid, close pressure valve to Air Tight and set the Cook Time for 5 minutes. Once cooking time has elapsed, immediately release the pressure and serve hot with white or yellow rice!

Spicy Lamb Meatballs

Prep Time: 20 minutes   Ready in: 45 hour   Yield: 10-20

INGREDIENTS

Sauce:
1 Cup Greek Yogurt
1/2 Cup english cucumber; peeled, seeded, finely chopped.
½ tsp garlic powder
1/3 cup fresh mint; chopped

Meatballs:
1 1/2 lb. ground lean lamb
1 1/2 tsp ground cumin
1 tsp ground coriander
1 clove garlic; minced
1 small white onion; minced
1/3 Cup fresh parsley; minced
1/2 small red pepper; minced
1 jalapeno; seeds and memberane removed; minced
1 lemon (zest and juice)
1 large egg; beaten
1/2 Cup dried bread crumbs
1 Cup water

DIRECTIONS

1. Make the Yogurt Sauce first and place into the refrigerator until ready to serve.
2. Make the meatballs by putting the meat into a large bowl. Blend in the minced onion, pepper, garlic, seasonings and lemon (juice and zest). Add the eggs and the bread crumbs. Using your hands, gently incorporate all the ingredients together and then form 1 1/2- 2" inch meatballs; set aside.
3. Place pressure cooker on a level surface, insert the pot and plug in. Set pressure cooking time to 15 minutes; press Start. Add olive oil to the pot. When oil is hot add a single layer of meatballs to the bottom of the pan. Use long tongs and brown on all sides. Remove to a paper towel. Brown the remaining meatballs in batches to prevent overcrowding. When the last batch is finished, pour in the water and scrape the bottom of the pan to loosen any stuck on bits.   Put the meatballs back into the cooker. Secure the lid, turn pressure valve to Air Tight.
4. When the cooking time has elapsed turn the keep warm feature off and let pressure release naturally.
5. Serve with the sauce as an appetizer or as an entree.

Beef LoMein

Prep Time: 5 minutes   Ready In:20 minutes   Yield: 4-6

INGREDIENTS
1 1/2 lb. flank steak
1 Tbsp sesame oil
1 medium onion; coarsely chopped
1 medium red pepper; coarsely chopped
1 medium green pepper; coarsely chopped
1 Cup snow peas (optional)
1 10.5 ounce can double strength beef broth
1/2 Cup water
¼ Cup low-sodium soy sauce
1 tsp ground ginger
2 cloves garlic; chopped
1 lb. lo mein noodles or spaghetti (broken in half)

DIRECTIONS
1. Cut flank steak into 3 length-wise pieces, then into ½" strips. Prepare all vegetables as directed above.
2. Place the pressure cooker on a level surface, inset the pan and plug in.   Press the preprogrammed Brown button or set Cook Time for 5 minutes and press Start. Add the sesame oil.
3. When the oil is hot, add the meat and quickly sauté 3-4 minutes or until it begins to brown. Add the vegetables and stir constantly until they are hot.
4. Add the remaining ingredients (except the noodles) and stir well. When the mixture comes to a boil, stir in the pasta.
5. Quickly secure lid onto the pressure cooker, set pressure valve to Air Tight.   Set Cook Time to 7 minutes. After the cooking time has elapsed, immediately release the pressure. Remove the lid and stir.
6. If the pasta isn't done or too much liquid remains, replace lid and turn the cooker to Keep Warm until desired texture is reached.

CHILI MAC

Prep Time: 15 minutes   Ready in: 1 hour   Yield: 10-12 servings

INGREDIENTS

1 1/2 lb. beef stew meat or beef chuck, cut into 1-inch cubes
1/2 Tbsp kosher salt
2 Tbsp vegetable oil
1 large Spanish onion; chopped
1 Cup green bell pepper; diced
2 cloves garlic; minced
1/4 Cup chili powder; use less or more depending on desired heat
1 Tbsp ground cumin
1 (15-ounce) can diced tomatoes; undrained
1 (8-ounce) can tomato sauce
1 (10-ounce) can Rotel® Tomatoes with chilies
3 Cups low-sodium chicken broth
1 lb. small elbow macaroni

DIRECTIONS

1. Wash and then pat dry the meat with a paper towel; season with the salt.
2. Place the pressure cooker on a level surface, insert the pot and plug in. Press the preprogrammed Brown button or set the Cook Time to 10 min.
3. Add 2 Tablespoons of oil to the pot and, when hot, add the meat, and cook 4-5 minutes or until well browned; add the garlic to the meat and cook for the last 2 minutes.
4. Add the remaining ingredients, except for the macaroni, and stir well.
5. Press Cancel and set Cook Time for 15 minutes; press Start. Secure the lid and turn the pressure valve to Air Tight.
6. When cooking time has elapsed, manually release the pressure and carefully open the lid. Stir in the macaroni.
7. Replace the lid, set valve to Air Tight, set Cook Time for 5 minutes and press Start.
8. When cooking time has elapsed, let pressure release naturally until you are able to safely remove the lid.
9. Stir well. Test the macaroni for doneness. If more time is needed, replace the lid and allow to cook on Keep Warm until tender.

TIP: ADD A CAN OF BUSHES CHILI BEANS IN SAUCE ALONG WITH THE MACARONI FOR A HEARTIER DISH.

RED MEATS

ITALIAN MEATBALLS IN SAUCE

Prep Time: 15 minutes   Ready in: 1 hour   Yield: 10-12 servings

INGREDIENTS
Sauce:
1 Cup onion; finely chopped
3 Tbsp olive oil
2- 29oz cans tomato sauce
2-28oz cans crushed tomatoes
2 Tbsp each dried oregano leaves, dried basil leaves, garlic salt and sugar
1 Tbsp dried thyme
½ tsp crushed red pepper flakes
½ tsp garlic powder
Meatballs:
1 lb. ground turkey
2 lb. ground extra lean beef
1 small onion; minced
1/2 small red pepper; minced
1 large eggs; beaten
3 cloves garlic
1 Tbs. each dried parsley flakes and. dried basil leaves
1/2 cup panko bread crumbs
1/2 cup grated Parmesan cheese

DIRECTIONS
1. Place pressure cooker on a level surface, insert the pot and plug in. Set pressure cooking time to 15 minutes; press Start.
2. Add olive oil to the pot. When oil is hot add the 1 cup of chopped onion and sauté for about 3 minutes. When the onion is tender, but not browned, add the canned tomatoes, the seasonings and the water.
3. Secure the lid, turn pressure valve to Air Tight.
4. When the cooking time has elapsed turn the keep warm feature off and let pressure release naturally.
5. While the sauce is cooking make the meatballs!
6. Put the meats together into a large bowl. Blend in the minced onion, pepper and garlic.
7. Add the eggs, the seasonings, the bread crumbs and the cheese.
8. Using your hands, gently incorporate all the ingredients together and form 1 1/2- 2" inch meatballs; set aside.

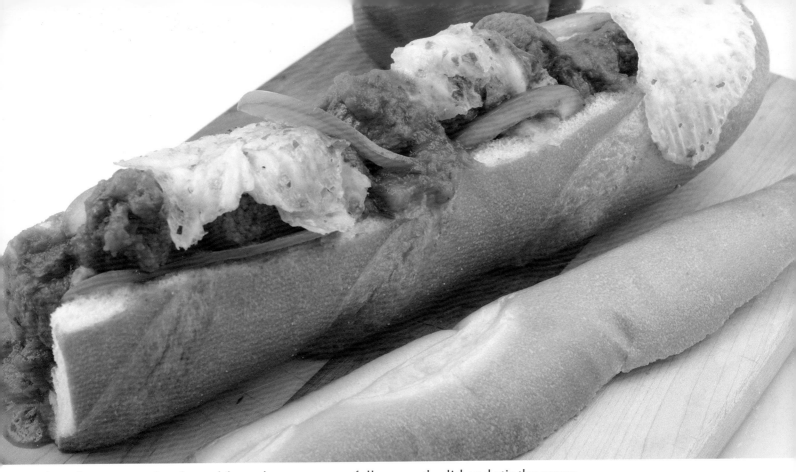

9. When the pressure is released from the sauce, carefully open the lid and stir the sauce.

10.Carefully drop the meatballs into the sauce, one by one, and stir gently. Replace the lid, set the valve to Air Tight and set cook time to 25 minutes; press Start.

11. When cooking time has elapsed turn the keep warm feature off and let stand for 5 minutes before moving the exhaust lever into the exhaust position.

12. Serve over spaghetti, your favorite pasta or make Hoagies!

COVER YOUR PRESSURE COOKER WITH A GLASS LID (OR USE THE PRESSURE LID WITH THE PRESSURE VALVE SET TO EXHAUST) AND USE THE KEEP WARM FEATURE TO KEEP THESE MEATBALLS PIPING HOT AND DELICIOUS DURING GET-TOGETHERS

SWISS STEAK & ONIONS

Prep Time: 10 minutes   Ready in: 50 minutes   Yield: 6

INGREDIENTS
¼ Cup olive oil
2 lb. beef round steak (1 ½ inches thick)
1 Cup flour
1 medium onion; diced
2 cloves garlic; minced
¼ Cup carrots; diced
1 bay leaf
1 tsp salt; divided
1 tsp pepper; divided
1 Cup beef broth
2 Tbsp Tomato paste
4-5 large onions; sliced into thick rings

DIRECTIONS
1. Place the steak into a baggie with the flour, 1/2 tsp salt and 1/2 tsp pepper and toss to coat.
2. Place the pressure cooker on a level surface, insert the pot and plug in.
3. Press the preprogrammed Brown button or set Cook Time for 5 minutes; press Start. Add the olive oil.
4. When the oil is hot, add the breaded meat to the pan (working in small batches so as not to overcrowd the pan) and fry 1-2 minutes on each side or until lightly browned. Remove meat and drain on paper towels. Repeat process until all the meat is cooked; add more oil as needed.
5. After the meat has been removed, add the diced onion, garlic, carrots, bay leaf, salt and pepper to the pan.
6. Sauté for just a minute and then add the beef broth, tomato paste and the browned steak pieces.
7. Secure lid onto the pressure cooker, set pressure valve to Air Tight.
8. Set Cook Time to 30 minutes. When the cooking time has elapsed, let the pressure release naturally for 5 minutes and the manually release remaining pressure.
9. Stir the mixture and add the onion rings to the top. Reposition the lid and set the timer for 5 minutes. Once cooking time has elapsed, press Cancel to turn of the Keep Warm feature and allow cooker to cool naturally until you can safely remove the lid.
10. Serve with hot buttered noodles or steamed white rice.

SLOPPY JOES

Prep Time: 5 minutes   Ready in: 40 minutes   Yield: 6-8 sandwiches

INGREDIENTS
2 Tbsp Olive oil
1 large onion; diced
1 clove garlic; minced
1 ½ lb. lean ground beef
¾ Cup beef broth
1 6-oz can tomato paste
2 Tbsp Light brown sugar
1 tsp Salt
½ tsp Chili powder
1 Tbsp Worcestershire sauce
Pinch crushed red pepper flakes

DIRECTIONS
1. Place the pressure cooker on a level surface, insert the pot and plug in.
2. Press the preprogrammed Brown button or set Cook Time for 5 minutes; press Start. Add the olive oil.
3. When the oil is hot, add and sauté the onion and garlic. Sauté about 3 minutes and then add the ground beef.
4. Cook for 2 minutes, stirring well to break up the meat. If the meat is fatty, carefully remove pot and pour the meat into a colander to strain and then return to pot. Add the remaining ingredients and stir well.
5. Secure the lid in place and set the pressure valve to Air Tight. Press Cancel and then select the preprogrammed Beef button or set the Cook Time to 30 minutes.
6. When cooking time has elapsed, unplug the pressure cooker and release pressure, manually or naturally, until lid can safely be removed.
7. Stir well and serve hot on rolls or buns.

STUFFED PEPPERS

Prep Time: 10 minutes   Ready in: 40 minutes   Yield: 5-6

INGREDIENTS

1 1/4 lb. lean ground beef
1 Cup onion; finely chopped
 1/2 tsp dried oregano leaves
1 tsp dried basil leaves
1/2 tsp garlic powder
1 tsp garlic salt
1 tsp dried thyme
1/2 plus 1 Cup spaghetti sauce, tomato sauce or tomato soup
2 Cups long grain rice
3 3/4 Cups water
5 Large bell peppers; any color
2-3 slices of American cheese

DIRECTIONS

1. Place pressure cooker on a level surface, insert the pot and plug in. Set press preprogrammed Rice button or set cook time to 12 minutes; press Start.
2. Add the ground beef and cook until browned. Add the onion and sauté for another 2 minutes. When the onion is tender stir in the seasonings and 1/2 Cup of the tomato sauce.
3. Add the rice and the water; stir well. Secure the lid, turn pressure valve to Air Tight.
4. When the cooking time has elapsed wait 5-7 minutes before manually releasing the pressure.
5. While the mixture is cooking, prepare the peppers. First, stand the peppers upright; and trim the bottom as necessary to keep the pepper from toppling over while cooking. Next, remove the top of the pepper and hollow out the membranes and seeds; discard.
6. When pressure is released, carefully remove the lid and stir the mixture well. Stuff the peppers.
7. Wash, rinse and dry the pressure pan; return to base. Pour the water into the bottom of the cooker.
8. Place the peppers into the pan. Attach the lid and set the exhaust valve to Air Tight. Set Cook Time to 5 minutes or press the preprogrammed Vegetable button.
9. When cooking time has elapsed, wait 3-5 minutes before releasing the pressure. Carefully remove the lid.
10. Evenly spoon the remaining 1 Cup tomato or spaghetti sauce over the stuffed peppers and top with cheese.
11. Return lid to cooker but leave valve on Exhaust. Let rest 5 minutes before serving. While the cheese is melting, reheat the remaining meat and rice mixture and serve with the peppers.

Beef & Mushroom Stroganoff

Prep Time: 5 minutes   Ready in: 35 minutes   Yield: 6-8 sandwiches

INGREDIENTS
1 Tbsp Vegetable oil
2 Tbsp butter
2 lb. beef tenderloin; trimmed and cut into 1- pieces
1 large onion; diced
1 lb. white mushrooms; washed and brushed; sliced
1 clove garlic; minced
1 tsp Salt
1 Tbsp Worcestershire sauce
1 Tbsp flour
1/2 Cup white wine
3 Cups beef stock
1 Cup sour cream
1 16-oz bag wide egg noodles

DIRECTIONS
1. Place the pressure cooker on a level surface, insert the pot and plug in.
2. Press the preprogrammed Beef button or set Cook Time for 15 minutes; press Start. Add the oil and 1 Tablespoon of the butter. When hot, add the beef and cook until the moisture is released. Drain beef into a colander, wipe out the pan and replace. Add the remaining butter to the pan.
3. When hot, add the onions, mushrooms and garlic. Add in the salt and the Worcestershire sauce. Sauté about 3 minutes and then sprinkle in the flour; cook about 1 minute and then slowly pour in the wine, stir until bubbly.
4. Add the beef and beef stock; stir well. Attach the lid and set the pressure valve to Air Tight. When cooking time has elapsed, press cancel and wait 7 minutes before manually releasing the pressure.
5. Open lid and stir well. Add in 16-oz wide egg noodles.   Attach the lid and set the pressure valve to Air Tight.
6. Set Cook Time for 5 minutes. Press Start.
7. When cooking time has elapsed, unplug the pressure cooker and release pressure, manually or naturally, until lid can safely be removed.
8. Stir in the sour cream. Heat through, toss and serve.

APRICOT PORK ROAST

Prep Time: 10 minutes Ready in: 45 minutes   Yield: 10-12

INGREDIENTS
1 2.5 - 3.5-lb. pork loin roast
1 Tbsp vegetable oil
1 ½ tsp salt
½ tsp coarse ground black pepper
1 Tbs fresh rosemary leaves; chopped
2 Tbsp Dijon mustard
1 Cup water
1 Tbsp honey
1 Tbsp brown sugar
1 Cup dried apricots; sliced
2 Tbsp water mixed with 2 Tbsp Corn Starch

DIRECTIONS
1. Place your pressure cooker on a level surface, insert the pressure pot, and plug the unit in.
2. Wash pork roast and pat dry. Make a paste with the salt, pepper, rosemary and mustard; rub the paste on the roast.
3. Set cook time to 30 minutes (or press Pork button) and press Start.
4. Add and when hot, use tongs to sear the edges of the roast on all sides.
5. Mix the apricot slices, honey and brown sugar into the water; pour over the top of the roast in the pot.
6. Attach the lid and set the pressure control to "air tight" or closed.
7. When cooking time has elapsed, manually release the pressure by opening the pressure control valve to exhaust
8. Once the pressure has been released, carefully open the lid and remove roast to a cutting board.
9. Press any preprogrammed button or set Cook Time to 5 minutes.
10. Mix the water with the corn starch to make a flurry. When the liquid in the pot begins to boil, stir in the flurry and turn off the pressure cooker.
11. Serve by slicing the roast and topping with the apricot mixture.

TIP: THIS RECIPE WILL RESULT IN A SLICEABLE ROAST. IF YOU PREFER A SHRED-ABLE ROAST, INCREASE THE COOKING TIME TO 45 MIN.

CHERRY PORT GLAZED PORK ROAST

Prep Time: 10 minutes   Ready in: 45 minutes   Yield: 10-12

INGREDIENTS
1 2.5 - 3.5-lb. pork loin roast
1 Tbsp olive oil
1 ½ tsp salt
1 tsp garlic powder
½ tsp coarse ground black pepper
1 Tbs fresh thyme or rosemary leaves; chopped
3/4 Cup ruby port
1/2 Cup Pie Filling
1/2 Cup water
2 Tbsp water mixed with 2 Tbsp Corn Starch

DIRECTIONS
1. Place your pressure cooker on a level surface, insert the pressure pot, and plug the unit in.
2. Wash pork roast and pat dry. Combine the salt, garlic powder, pepper and fresh thyme or rosemary; sprinkle evenly on the roast and rub in well..
3. Set cook time to 25 minutes (or press Pork button) and press Start.
4. Add olive oil and when hot, use tongs to sear the edges of the roast on all sides. About 1-2 min on each side.
5. Pour the port over the roast. Let the port wine cook down 5 minutes as you continue to turn the pork over.
6. Mix pie filling into the water; pour over the top of the roast in the pot.
7. Attach the lid and set the pressure control to "air tight" or closed.
8. When cooking time has elapsed, manually release the pressure by opening the pressure control valve to exhaust.
9. Once the pressure has been released, carefully open the lid and remove roast to a cutting board.
10. Press any preprogrammed button or set Cook Time to 5 minutes.
11. Mix the water with the corn starch to make a flurry. When the liquid in the pot begins to boil, stir in the flurry and turn off the pressure cooker.
12. Serve by slicing the roast and topping with the cherry mixture.

TIP: THIS RECIPE WILL RESULT IN A SLICEABLE ROAST. IF YOU PREFER A SHRED-ABLE ROAST, INCREASE THE COOKING TIME TO 45 MINUTES.

PORK

Sweet 'n Sour Pork Roast

Prep Time: 5 minutes   Ready in: 1 hour 15 minutes   Yield: allow 1/4 lb. per serving

INGREDIENTS
1 3-4 lb. boneless pork loin roast
1 Cup water
1 tsp each of salt & pepper
1 large onion; cut into large bite-sized chunky pieces
1 green pepper; cut into large bite-sized chunky pieces
1 red pepper; cut into large bite-sized chunky pieces
9 oz. Sweet 'n Sour sauce (I use World Harbors Maui Mountain
1 can pineapple chunks; drain but save the liquid
1 Tbsp corn starch

DIRECTIONS
1. Place pressure cooker on a level surface, insert the pot and plug in.
2. Sprinkle the roast with the salt and pepper and place into the pressure cooker pot with 1 cup water.
3. Secure lid and set the pressure valve to Air Tight (closed). Press the preprogrammed Pork button or set Cook Time to 30 minutes.
4. When the cook time has elapsed, press Cancel to turn off the machine. Place a cold damp towel over the top and wait 5 minutes. Allow pressure to drop (about 10 minutes) or gently toggle the pressure gauge and quick release the pressure until you can safely remove the lid.
5. Place the roast on a plate and drain the liquid from the pot. Return the roast to the pot and add the onion, peppers and drained pineapple.
6. In a medium bowl, whisk together 2 Tbsp of the pineapple juice and the corn starch. Whisk in the remaining pineapple juice and the sweet 'n sour sauce. Pour mixture over the roast and veggies.
7. Reattach lid, set valve to Air Tight and press the preprogrammed "Pork" button or set Cook Time to 30 minutes.
8. When the cooker switches to "keep warm" follow the same method above to release the pressure and remove the lid.
9. Slice and serve with white rice.

MOJO PORK

Prep Time: 5 minutes   Ready in: 17 minutes   Yield: 1 chop per serving

INGREDIENTS
1 C Extra virgin olive oil
1 tsp ground cumin
1 tsp salt
4 Tbs minced garlic
6 Tbs lime juice
6 Tbs orange juice
2 tsp oregano leaves
2 tsp lemon
1 Tbsp olive oil
1 sweet onion; coarsely chopped
1 3-lb. Boston butt roast
3/4 Cup Mojo marinade; store bought or homemade (recipe below)
1/4 Cup water
White rice (prepared as directed by package)

DIRECTIONS
1. Make the marinade by whisking together the first 8 ingredients; set aside until ready to use.
2. Place your pressure cooker on a level surface, insert the pressure pot, and plug the unit in.
3. Wash pork roast and pat dry; set aside.
4. Set cook time to 70 mins and press Start.
5. Add oil and when hot, add onion.
6. Brown for 2-3 minutes or until onions soften.
7. Using long tongs carefully lower roast into the pot.
8. Add water and mojo sauce and using the tongs, turn the roast in the liquid until all sides are coated.
9. Attach the lid and set the pressure control to "air tight" or closed.
10. When cooking time has elapsed, manually release the pressure by opening the pressure control valve to exhaust.
11. Once the pressure has been released, carefully open the lid and remove roast to a cutting board.
12. Use two forks to shred the pork and then place back into the pot, toss with the sauce and onions.
13. Close lid, leaving the valve on exhaust and unit on Keep Warm function until ready to serve.

THIS DISH IS TRADITIONALLY SERVED WITH WHITE OR YELLOW RICE, BLACK BEANS AND CHOPPED ONION.
COMPLETE THE MEAL WITH FRIED PLAINTAINS AND SANGRIA AND YOU'LL THINK YOU WERE IN CUBA!

BARBECUE PORK PULL-APART

Prep Time: 5 minutes   Ready in: 1 hour 25 minutes   Yield: 12 servings or sandwiches

INGREDIENTS
3 ½ lb. pork shoulder blade roast; wash and pat dry
1 16-oz. can or bottle beer
1 Cup water
1 Tbsp liquid smoke
1 tsp onion salt
1 tsp Kosher salt
1 tsp coarse ground pepper
1 18-oz. bottle barbecue sauce (your favorite brand)

DIRECTIONS
1. Place pressure cooker on a level surface, insert the pot and plug in .
2. Pour beer, water and the next 4 seasonings into the pot. Stir and allow bubbles to subside. Add washed pork roast.
3. Secure lid, set the pressure valve to Air Tight (closed) and set timer for 1 hour 15 minutes. Press Start.
4. When cook time has elapsed, release pressure.
5. Remove roast from pan and place onto a cutting board. Discard liquid in the pot.
6. Remove bone and any large fat portions from roast; discard. Using two large forks, shred meat; or chop if you prefer. You may serve immediately, as is, or drizzle barbecue on each serving. To serve later, return meat to pan and stir in BBQ sauce, mixing well.
7. Set the pressure cooker to Keep Warm. Cover, leaving pressure valve at Exhaust, and serve when desired. You may need to add additional BBS sauce or 1/4 C water to keep the meat moist until you are ready to serve.

SERVE ON BUNS WITH ADDITIONAL SAUCE, DILL PICKLE SLICES AND THINLY SLICED ONION!

TV Tidbit - When showing this delicious dish on live TV, it's always a little scary for the on-air guest when they are first "pulling" the roast. A big blob of fat, a string that was forgotten to be removed or worse, a super-tough piece of meat that just won't shred! Although the PC makes is virtually impossible to mess up, it can (and does) happen. If you were unlucky enough to get an overly lean, tough cut of meat, try it again...its usually perfect!

PORK CHOPS AND APPLESAUCE

Prep Time: 5 minutes   Ready in: 30 minutes   Yield: 4 servings

INGREDIENTS

4 medium pork loin chops (boneless) about ½ inch thick
3 Tbsp vegetable oil
1 tsp salt
1 tsp coarse ground pepper
3 Tbsp butter
1 shallot; finely chopped
1 clove garlic; minced
2 tsp balsamic vinegar
1 Tbsp dried rosemary
1 heaping tablespoon light brown sugar
1 1/4 Cups apple cider
2 large granny smith apples, peeled, cored and cut into thick slices

DIRECTIONS

1. Wash, pat dry, salt and pepper pork chops.
2. Place pressure cooker on a level surface, insert the pan and plug in. Select the browning feature or set Cook Time to 8 minutes.
3. Add the oil and, when hot, brown the chops on both sides and then drain on paper towels.
4. Pour off about half of the oil. Add butter, shallots and garlic; cook gently for about 1 minute. Add the vinegar and scrape the bottom of the pan with a spatula.
5. Add the rosemary, brown sugar and apple cider; stir well. Place chops back in pot.
6. Attach lid and set pressure valve to Airtight (closed). Press Cancel and set Cook Time for 10 minutes (or press the preprogrammed pork button) and press Start.
7. When cooking time has elapsed, release pressure and carefully remove lid. Turn the chops over and top with the apple slices. Reattach lid, close the regulator valve and set cook time for 4 minutes. Press Start.
8. When cooking time has elapsed, release pressure and carefully remove lid.
9. Remove the chops to a plate; cover with foil to keep warm. To serve the apples, they can be further mashed, stirred into the liquid or removed with a slotted spoon and served on the chops.

BLACKBERRY BALSAMIC PORK-CHOPS

Prep Time: 5 minutes   Ready in: 20 minutes   Yield: 1 chop per serving

INGREDIENTS

1-4 Center-cut pork loin chops (bone-in 3/4 in thick)
1 Tbsp Olive oil
1/2 tsp salt
1/2 tsp pepper
1 Tbsp Fresh rosemary; chopped
3/4 Cup water
1 tsp Dijon mustard
2 1/2 Tbsp balsamic vinegar
2/3 Cup fresh blackberries (about 20)
Slurry (2 Tbsp cold water + 2 tsp corn starch)

DIRECTIONS

1. Place your pressure cooker on a level surface, insert the pressure pot, and plug the unit in.
2. Set cook time to 10 mins and press Start.
3. Wash pork-chops and pat dry. Lightly season both sides with salt, fresh-ground black pepper and rosemary.
4. Add olive oil to the pan and when oil is hot, add pork-chops.
5. Cook 2-3 minutes each side or until they begin to brown.
6. While pork-chops are browning, stir the dijon mustard into the 3/4 Cups water.
7. When pork-chops have browned, add the balsamic vinegar followed by the water and mustard mixture.
8. Attach the lid of your pressure cooker and set the pressure control to "air tight" or closed.
9. When cooking time has elapsed, manually release the pressure by opening the pressure control valve to exhaust.
10. Carefully open the lid and remove pork-chops to a plate and cover with foil to keep warm.
11. Press the Cancel button and reset cook time to 4 minutes; press Start.
12. When remaining mixture begins to boil add the slurry and the blackberries; stir well
13. Let sauce cook for 2-3 minutes or until thickened.
14. Serve immediately over pork-chops.

GINGER PORK STIR FRY

Prep Time: 10 minutes   Ready in: 30 minutes   Yield: 4-6

INGREDIENTS
10 oz. pork loin roast; trimmed and cut into bite-sized pieces
1 Tbsp vegetable oil
1 ½ tsp salt
1/2 tsp Paprika
2 tsp sesame oil
1 medium orange bell pepper; thinly sliced
1 Cup snow peas
1/2 Cup julienned celery
1 Tbsp minced peeled fresh ginger
3 Tbsp rice vinegar
1 Tbsp soy sauce
2 tsp sugar
1 tsp chili garlic sauce
2 Cups chicken broth
8 oz angel hair or thin spaghetti noodles

DIRECTIONS
1. Place your pressure cooker on a level surface, insert the pressure pot, and plug the unit in.
2. Wash pork roast and pat dry. Cut into bite-sized pieces and toss with the salt and paprika.
3. Set cook time to 7 minutes (or press Pork button and adjust time) and press Start.
4. Add olive oil and when hot, use tongs to sear the pork cubes. About 1-2 min on each side.
5. Remove pork to platter. Add the sesame oil to the pot and add the bell pepper, snow peas, celery and ginger.
6. Add the pork, stir fry for about 1 minute and then add the chicken broth, vinegar, soy sauce, sugar and garlic sauce. Stir well.
7. Break the pasta in half and add it to the pot. Use a fork to seperate the noodles.
8. Attach the lid and set the pressure control to "air tight" or closed.
9. When cooking time has elapsed, manually release the pressure by opening the pressure control valve to exhaust.
10. Once the pressure has been released, carefully open the lid and toss.
11. Serve immediately.

TV Tidbit - When making dishes like this on TV, the snow peas and the orange pepper would not be cooked but rather tossed in at the end to give fresh, vibrant color!

Pork Chops With Olives

Prep Time: 7 minutes   Ready in: 13 minutes   Yield: 1 chop per serving

INGREDIENTS
1-4 Center-cut pork loin chops (bone-in 3/4 in thick)
1/4 Cup onions; diced
1 large clove of garlic; minced
1 (14.5 oz) can of petite diced tomatoes
2 bay leaves
1/2 Cup small green pimento stuffed olives; chopped
1 Tbsp Olive oil
1/2 tsp salt
1/2 tsp pepper

DIRECTIONS
1. Place your pressure cooker on a level surface, insert the pressure pot, and plug the unit in.
2. Set cook time to 10 mins and press Start.
3. Wash pork-chops and pat dry. Lightly season both sides with salt, fresh-ground black pepper.
4. Add olive oil to the pan and when oil is hot, add onions.
5. Cook for 1 minute, stirring constantly and then add pork-chops
6. Cook for 2 minutes and turn the pork-chops over.
7. Add minced garlic into sizzling onions; stir well and cook another 2 minutes.
8. Add tomatoes, 2 bay leaves and olives; stir gently.
9. Attach the lid and set the pressure control to "air tight" or closed.
10. When cooking time has elapsed, manually release the pressure by opening the pressure control valve to exhaust.
11. Carefully open lid and serve immediately.

Tip: Serve with white or yellow rice and a cold, green salad.

TURKEY BREAST

Prep Time: 15 minutes   Ready in: 45 minutes   Yield: 6-8 servings

INGREDIENTS
1 Tbsp vegetable oil
1 6-7 lb. bone-in, skin on turkey breast
1 tsp salt
1/4 tsp dried thyme leaves
1/4 tsp paprika
2 Cups chicken or turkey broth
1 medium-large white onion; quartered
2 stalks celery with leaves; cut into 2" pieces
7-8 baby carrots
2 Tbsp butter
2 Tbsp flour

DIRECTIONS
1. Place your pressure cooker on a level surface, insert the pressure pot and plug the unit in.
2. Wash turkey and pat dry. Mix the salt, paprika and thyme together in a small bowl. Sprinkle the seasoning on the turkey skin and rub in well. Set aside. Wash and prep the veggies; set aside.
3. Set Cook Time to 25 minutes or press the Meat button and increase time to 25 minutes. Press Start.
4. Add the oil to the pan and when hot stir in the onion, celery and carrots. Cook for 3-4 minutes and push to the side.
5. Using tongs (or your hands if you are careful) place the turkey, breast down, into the pan. Cook 1-2 minutes, rotating as needed, until the top is lightly browned. Pour chicken broth around the chicken.
6. Check that cook time is at 25 min or adjust as needed. Attach the lid and turn the pressure valve to Air Tight.
7. When the cook time has elapsed, allow the cooker to rest 10 minutes before manually exhausting the remaining pressure. Carefully open the lid. Transfer Turkey Breast to a carving board. Cover loosely with aluminum foil and let rest.

Make the Gravy: Place a small colander over a large measuring cup; drain the hot broth and vegetables. Save 2 Cups of broth to make the gravy. The veggies will be overcooked but can be eaten or blended into the broth.
   • Press the preprogrammed Brown button or set cook time to 10 minutes.
   • Add the butter to the pan. When almost melted, sprinkle in the flour and cook to make a paste; about 2 minutes. Slowly add the broth and bring to boil. Reduce the temperature and simmer until thick. Serve hot over the turkey slices!

Spanish Chicken

Prep Time: 5 minutes   Ready in: 40 minutes   Yield: 4 servings

INGREDIENTS
2 Tbsp Olive oil.
1 medium yellow onion; sliced into thick rings
3 cloves garlic; minced
4 frozen boneless, skinless chicken breasts (about 1 to 1 1/3 lb.)
1 28-oz can crushed tomatoes
¼ tsp salt
1 bay leaf
10 large Spanish olives; cut in half

DIRECTIONS
1. Place your pressure cooker on a level surface, insert the pressure pot and plug the unit in.
2. Set cook time to 15 min or select the preprogrammed Chicken button; press Start.
3. Add the olive oil and when hot, add the onion and garlic. Sauté for 1-2 minutes and then stir in the tomatoes, salt, bay leaf and olives.
4. Use tongs and place the frozen chicken into the sauce.
5. Attach the lid and turn the pressure valve to Air Tight.
6. When the machine switches to "keep warm" in about 20 minutes, turn the machine off. Place a cold damp towel over the top and wait 5 minutes. Allow pressure to drop (about 10 minutes) or gently toggle the pressure gauge and quick release the pressure until you can safely remove the lid.
7. Serve with yellow or white rice.

TV Tidbit - Doing a frozen-chicken demo during a TV shopping presentation of the Elite pressure cooker, has been popular for many years because it really works! This recipe uses tomatoes and is served over rice but you can vary it by using salsa and serving chicken tacos or using cream of mushroom soup and serving over noodles. The possibilties are endless! Have fun and make up your own "demos"!

TIME SAVER TIP: SUBSITUTE THAWED CHICKEN AND THE COOK TIME WILL AUTOMATICALLY BE
REDUCED BY ABOUT 5-8 MINUTES BECAUSE THE COOKER WILL COME TO PRESSURE FASTER!

Easy Chicken & Dumplings

Prep Time: 20 minutes   Ready in: 35 minutes   Yield: 4-6 servings

INGREDIENTS

3 Tbsp butter
½ Cup diced carrot
¼ Cup diced celery
¼ Cup flour
4 Cups chicken broth
1-1½ lbs boneless, skinless chicken breasts
½ tsp salt
¼ tsp pepper
¼ tsp poultry seasoning
2 -7.5 oz. Cans biscuits, pressed slightly flat & cut into 4 strips per biscuit.

DIRECTIONS

1. Wash, pat dry and cut chicken into bite-sized pieces. Sprinkle with the salt and pepper and set aside.
2. Open the cans of biscuits and lay them out onto a cutting board. Press each biscuit semi-flat and then cut into 1" wide strips. Set aside.
3. Place your pressure cooker on a level surface, and plug the unit in.
4. Set Cook Time to 20 min or select the Chicken setting; press Start.
5. When the pot begins to heat up add butter. Stir in the carrots and celery and cook until lightly browned.
6. Add the flour and stir in well. Cook for 1 to 2 minutes or until it is beginning to brown. If the flour is not quite moist enough add a little of the chicken broth at this time.
7. Stir in the chicken broth, cubed chicken breasts and seasonings.
8. Slowly drop the canned biscuits into the mixture using a spoon to gently push biscuits into broth so that each biscuit piece has been coated.
9. Attach the lid and set the pressure valve to Air Tight.
10. When the pressure cooker switches to "keep warm", unplug the machine and let the pressure slowly drop until no pressure remains. Open lid, stir well, close the lid and let rest 5 minutes before serving.

THIS RECIPE IS THE FASTEST WAY TO A CHICKEN AND DUMPLING DINNER! YOU CAN DOUBLE OR TRIPLE THIS RECIPE TO FEED A HUNGRY CROWD. IF YOU HAVE EXTRA TIME, PREPARE A WHOLE CHICKEN AND USE THE SHREDDED MEAT RATHER THAN THE BREASTS. IT GIVES THE DISH AN EXTRA DEPTH OF FLAVOR THAT THE BREASTS LACK.

CHICKEN 'N RICE

Prep Time: 5 minutes   Ready in: 25 minutes   Yield: 4 servings

INGREDIENTS
3 Tbsp vegetable oil
1 ½ lb. boneless skinless chicken breast; cut into bite-sized pieces
½ medium onion; minced
1 cup baby carrots; minced
¼ tsp Garlic powder
1 tsp salt
1/2 tsp fresh ground black pepper
3 Cups long grain white rice
6 Cups chicken broth

DIRECTIONS
1. Place your pressure cooker on a level surface, insert the pressure pot and plug the unit in.
2. Set cook time to 12 min or select the preprogrammed Rice button; press Start.
3. Add the oil and when hot, add the onion and sauté for 1-2 minutes. Add the carrots and sauté another 2 minutes.
4. Add the broth, salt, pepper and chicken pieces and bring to a boil.
5. Stir in the rice.
6. Attach the lid and turn the pressure valve to Air Tight.
7. When the machine switches to "keep warm" in about 15 minutes, press Cancel to turn the machine off.
8. Allow pressure to drop naturally for about 10 minutes and then or gently toggle the pressure gauge and quick release the remaining pressure until you can safely remove the lid.

IF YOU PREFER TO USE BROWN RICE, ADJUST THE COOK TIME TO 16 MINUTES OR CHOOSE THE BROWN RICE PREPROGRAMMED BUTTON.

Buffalo-Style Chicken Wings
Prep Time: 5 minutes   Ready in: 25 minutes   Yield: 4 servings

INGREDIENTS
5-20 pounds of chicken wings;
      I buy the frozen, sectioned wings and do not use the tips.
1-2 tsp. salt
1 bottle of wing sauce; I like Crystal but you can use your favorite.

DIRECTIONS
1. Place your pressure cooker on a level surface, insert the pressure pot and plug the unit in.
2. Place the wings in a colander, 5 pounds at a time, and with cold water running over them, use your hands to wash each one. Place them on a cookie sheet lined with paper towels and pat dry.
3. Sprinkle lightly with salt and place into the cooker. Pour 1/2 C wing sauce over the wings and use your hands again to mix well.
4. Repeat these steps until you have as many wings in the pot as you would like... up to 20 pounds.
5. Set Cook Time for 15 minutes and press Start.
6. Attach the lid and set the exhaust valve to the Air Tight (closed) position and let cook.
7. When the cooking time has elapsed, unplug or remove from heat and let the cooker rest for 5 minutes before manually releasing the pressure. Carefully open the lid.
8. Turn your oven onto the High Broil setting or preheat your grill.
9. If you are cooking only 5 pounds of wings, carefully drain the liquid from the wings and spread out onto a non-stick cookie sheet. If you have a full pot of wings, use a slotted spoon to place the wings on the cookie sheet. DO NOT try to drain and entire pot of wings...it is heavy and the steam will burn you!
10. Serve the wings hot, with the remaining wing sauce on a platter with celery sticks and either ranch or blue cheese dressing.

TV Tidbit - The Chicken Wing demo was started by Marc Gill using the Elite 8 qt PC. It's a great way to cook a lot of wings fast but I highly reccommend browning them before serving because they look better on-air than they taste!

Tasty Tip:

After pressure cooking, crisp the wings before serving! Simply place the wings in a single layer, on a nonstick pan.

Place under the broiler, on a middle rack. Cook 3-5 minutes or until they are beginning to crisp.

Turn wings over and brown the other side. Baste with wing sauce as desired.

CHICKEN WITH RASPBERRY GLAZE

rep Time: 10 minutes   Ready in: 30 minutes   Yield: 4-6 servings

INGREDIENTS
4 skinless, boneless chicken breast halves
½ teaspoon salt
¼ teaspoon pepper
2 tablespoons butter
2 tablespoon vegetable oil
6 green onions (scallions); chopped
1/3 cup raspberry vinegar
½ cup chicken broth
1/3 cup heavy cream
1 tablespoon Dijon mustard
1 cup fresh or frozen raspberries

DIRECTIONS
1. Wash, pat dry and season the chicken with the salt and pepper.
2. Place your pressure cooker on a level surface, insert the pressure pot and plug the unit in. Set Cook Time to 15 minutes or press the preprogrammed Chicken button and adjust time from there. Press Start.
3. Add 1 Tbsp butter and 1 Tbsp vegetable oil to the pot. When hot, add the chicken, without overlapping, and cook, turning once, until both sides are lightly browned; 3-4 minutes. Remove to a plate.
4. Add the remaining butter and oil. Sauté the scallions, 1-2 minutes, until soft and fragrant.
5. Stir in the vinegar, chicken broth and mustard. Return the chicken to the pot.
6. Attach the lid and turn the pressure valve to Air Tight.
7. When the cook time has elapsed, manually release the pressure. Carefully open the lid.
8. Remove chicken to a plate and cover with foil.

Make the sauce -
9. The cooker should be on Keep Warm but if not, set Cook Time to 5 minutes.
10. Bring liquid to a boil and stir in the cream. Simmer 2-3 minutes, until sauce slightly thickens.
11. Return chicken to pan. Add the raspberries and stir gently. Cook until heated through; 1 minute.
12. To serve, arrange the chicken on a warm platter and pour the sauce over all.

CHICKEN TACOS

Prep Time: 15 minutes   Ready in: 25 minutes   Yield: 10-12

INGREDIENTS

6 6-oz frozen or thawed boneless skinless chicken
    breast halves (about 2 pounds)
2 Cups chicken broth
1 1/2 tsp cumin divided
1/2-tsp onion salt
1 medium onion; diced
1-Tbsp olive oil
1/4-tsp cayenne pepper
1 4-oz. can chopped green chilies
1 5.5-oz. can spicy V-8 juice
12 soft tortillas or 12 hard taco shells (or combo thereof)
Optional Toppings: lettuce, shredded Cheddar or Jack cheese, sour cream, salsa, sliced jalapeños

DIRECTIONS

1. Place your pressure cooker on a level surface, insert the pressure pot and plug the unit in.
2. Set cook time to 20 min or select the preprogrammed Chicken button; press Start.
3. Pour the chicken broth into the pot and stir in 1 teaspoon cumin and the onion salt; bring to a boil.
4. Use tongs and add the chicken breasts.
5. Attach the lid and turn the pressure valve to Air Tight.
6. When the cooking time has elapsed, allow pressure to release naturally until no pressure remains and you can open the lid.   Remove the chicken to a cutting board and strain the hot liquid into a large bowl or measuring cup. Cut each breast in half, widthwise and use forks and pull the breasts apart. Place into the liquid.
7. Wipe the pressure pot clean, place into the base. Set the Cook Time for 10 minutes and press Start. Add the olive oil to the pan. When hot, add the onions and cook for 3-4 minutes or until onions begin to brown and then stir in the remaining 1/2 teaspoon cumin, the cayenne pepper and the can of chopped green chilies.
8. Use tongs and add the wet pulled chicken to the pan; do not add any extra liquid other than what clings to the chicken.
9. Stir the mixture well and then pour the spicy V-8 juice over all. Cook until the mixture is heated through, close the lid leaving the exhaust valve open (or use the glass lid) and switch the cooker to keep warm. Simmer 5 minutes or until you are ready to serve.
10. Serve on warm tortillas or taco shells and top with optional toppings above.

Lemony Chicken

Prep Time: 10 minutes   Ready in: 25 minutes   Yield: 4-6 servings

INGREDIENTS

4 skinless, boneless chicken breast halves
2-oz very thinly sliced prosciutto
2 Tbs plus 1/4 Cup lemon juice
lemon wedges
½ tsp salt
¼ tsp pepper
1/4 tsp thyme
2 Tbsp olive oil
½ Cup chicken broth
1 tsp cornstarch

DIRECTIONS

1. Wash, pat dry and season the chicken with the salt, pepper and thyme. Carefully wrap the chicken breasts with the prosciutto. If necessary, secure with toothpick.
2. Place your pressure cooker on a level surface, insert the pressure pot and plug the unit in. Set Cook Time to 15 minutes or press the preprogrammed Chicken button and adjust time from there. Press Start.
3. Add the olive oil to the pot. When hot, add the chicken, without overlapping, and cook, turning once, until both sides are lightly browned; 3-4 minutes. Remove to a plate.
4. Add the chicken broth and 2 Tbsp of the lemon juice; scrape the bottom of the pan.
5. Return the chicken to the pot. Attach the lid and turn the pressure valve to Air Tight.
6. When the cook time has elapsed, manually release the pressure. Carefully open the lid.
7. Remove chicken to a plate and cover with foil.
8. Make the sauce by selecting the brown button or set Cook Time to 5 minutes.
9. Mix the cornstarch into the remaining lemon juice and pour into the boiling liquid. Simmer 2-3 minutes, until sauce slightly thickens.
10. To serve, arrange the chicken on a warm platter and pour the sauce over all.

CURRIED APRICOT CHICKEN

Prep Time: 15 minutes   Ready in: 45 minutes   Yield: 6-8 servings

INGREDIENTS
1 3½-4 lb whole chicken
4 Tbsp apricot all-fruit or preserves
2 tsp curry powder
½ tsp ground coriander
½ tsp ground ginger
¼ tsp salt
1 Cup chicken broth
1 medium onion; quartered
2 medium cloves garlic
3-4 Cups cooked long grain rice
18" length of heavy-duty aluminum foil

DIRECTIONS
1. Place your pressure cooker on a level surface, insert the pressure pot and plug the unit in.
2. Fold the aluminum foil in half lengthwise and place into the bottom of the pressure pot. This will act as a sling to help you remove the chicken after cooking.
3. Wash chicken and pat dry. Place the onion wedges and the whole garlic cloves into the cavity of the chicken. Set chicken into the pressure cooker on top of the aluminum foil.
4. In a small bowl combine the apricot all-fruit, curry powder, coriander, ginger and salt to make a thin paste.
5. Mix 1 Tbsp of the paste into the chicken broth and pour around the chicken. Use a basting brush and thoroughly coat the chicken with the remaining paste.
6. Set cook time to 25 min or select the preprogrammed Chicken button; press Start. Attach the lid and turn the pressure valve to Air Tight.
7. When the cook time has elapsed, press Cancel to turn the machine off and manually release the pressure. Carefully open the lid. Use the aluminum foil to transfer the chicken from the pan to a plate. Loosely cover with foil to keep warm.
8. Make the sauce: Separate the fat from the liquid in the pan; discard fat. Remove onions and garlic from the cavity of the chicken and place in a food processor or blender with the separated liquid; process until smooth. Form a paste by heating 2 tablespoons butter and 2 tablespoons flour in a small saucepan over medium heat (or you may use the Brown setting on your pressure cooker). Slowly pour in the processed liquid and bring to a gentle boil for 2-3 three minutes until thick and bubbly.
9. Slice the chicken and drizzle the sauce over the slices.

40 Clove Chicken

Prep Time: 15 minutes   Ready in: 45 minutes   Yield: 6-8 servings

INGREDIENTS
1 Tbsp olive oil
1 3½-4 lb whole chicken
¼ tsp salt
1 Cup chicken broth
2 lemons; 1 halved and 1 sliced
1 medium onion; quartered
10 medium cloves garlic; each sliced into 4 pieces

18″ length of heavy-duty aluminum foil

DIRECTIONS
1. Place your pressure cooker on a level surface, insert the pressure pot and plug the unit in.
2. Fold the aluminum foil in half lengthwise and set aside until it is time to place it into the bottom of the pressure pot. This will act as a sling to help you remove the chicken after cooking.
3. Set the Cook Time for 25 minutes; press Start.
4. Wash chicken and pat dry. Sprinkle with the salt and pepper.
5. When the oil is hot, place the chicken into the pan, breast down and sear for 1-2 minutes on all sides. Remove chicken to a plate. Add the garlic and lemon slices into the pan. Saute quickly for about 1 minute just to release the flavors. Use tongs or a spoon to place the lemon and garlic into the chicken cavity. Add chicken broth.
6. Set chicken into the pressure cooker on top of the aluminum foil.
7. In a small bowl combine the apricot all-fruit, curry powder, coriander, ginger and salt to make a thin paste.
8. Attach the lid and turn the pressure valve to Air Tight.
9. When the cook time has elapsed, press Cancel to turn the machine off and manually release the pressure. Carefully open the lid. Use the aluminum foil to transfer the chicken from the pan to a plate. Loosely cover with foil to keep warm until ready to serve.

TIP: PLACE THE CHICKEN UNDER THE BROILER OF YOUR OVEN TO CRISP THE SKIN.
OTHERWISE, REMOVE AND DISCARD THE SKIN BEFORE SERVING. SERVE WITH A CRISP CESAR SALAD.

Chicken Breasts with Artichokes, Cream & Tomatoes

Prep Time: 10 minutes   Ready in: 40 minutes   Yield: 6 servings

INGREDIENTS
6 chicken breasts; boneless, skinless
1 ½ tsp salt
½ tsp pepper
2 Tbsp olive oil
1 Tbsp butter
1 small onion; finely chopped
1 Cup dry white wine
1 Cup chicken broth
1 Tbsp granulated chicken bouillon
1 14 ½ oz. can diced tomatoes, drained
1 10 oz. can artichoke hearts; drained and quartered lengthwise
1 ½ Cups heavy cream
2 Tbsp chopped fresh basil

DIRECTIONS
1. Rinse chicken and pat dry. Season with half of the salt and pepper.
2. Place your pressure cooker on a level surface, insert the pressure pot and plug the unit in.
3. Set cook time to 12 min or select the preprogrammed Chicken button; press Start.
4. Add the oil and when hot, add the chicken breasts and sauté 3-4 minutes or until lightly browned on both sides.
5. Add the butter, onion, wine, chicken broth and bouillon; bring to a boil. Attach the lid and turn the pressure valve to Air Tight.
6. When the cook time has elapsed, press Cancel to turn the machine off and manually release the pressure. Carefully open the lid. Turn the chicken over and add the drained tomatoes and artichokes. Reattach lid, turn the pressure valve to Air Tight and set Cook Time for 2 minutes; press Start.
7. When cook time has elapsed, press Cancel to turn off the Keep Warm function and manually release the pressure. Carefully open the lid.
8. Remove the chicken to a plate and cover to keep warm. Set the cook time for 10 minutes and press Start.
9. Once the mixture boils, switch the pressure cooker to Keep Warm, add cream and basil; simmer slowly for 5-8 minutes or until just about 2 cups liquid remains.
10. Taste the sauce and add the remaining salt and pepper if desired. Return chicken to pan, cover with glass lid (or use pressure lid with valve set to Exhaust) and heat together for about 5 minutes.

Cajun Turkey Breast
Prep Time: 15 minutes   Ready in: 45 minutes   Yield: 6-8 servings

INGREDIENTS
1 Tbsp vegetable oil
1 6-7 lb. bone-in, skin on turkey breast
2 Tbsp kosher salt
1 Tbsp cayenne pepper
1 Tbsp garlic powder
2 Tbsp sweet paprika
1 Tbsp dried oregano
1 Tbsp dried thyme
1 Tbsp freshly ground black pepper
1 Tbsp onion powder
1 medium-large white onion; quartered
1 medium green pepper; quartered; seeds and membranes removed
1 Cups chicken or turkey broth

DIRECTIONS
1. Place your pressure cooker on a level surface, insert the pressure pot and plug the unit in.
2. Wash turkey and pat dry. Wash and prep the veggies; set aside.
3. Mix the salt, cayenne, garlic powder, paprika, oregeno, thyme pepper and onion powder together in a small bowl. Sprinkle the seasoning on the turkey skin and rub in well. Set aside.
4. Set Cook Time to 30 minutes or press the Meat button and increase time to 30 minutes. Press Start.
5. Add the oil to the pan and when hot stir in the onion and peppers. Cook for 3-4 minutes and push to the side.
6. Using tongs (or your hands if you are careful) place the turkey, breast down, into the pan. Cook 1-2 minutes, rotating as needed, until the top is lightly browned. Pour chicken broth around the chicken.
7. Check that cook time remains at 30 min or adjust as needed. Attach the lid and turn the pressure valve to Air Tight.
8. When the cook time has elapsed, allow the cooker to rest 10 minutes before manually exhausting the remaining pressure. Carefully open the lid. Transfer Turkey Breast to a carving board. Cover loosely with aluminum foil and let rest.

TIP: PLACE THE TURKEY BREAST UNDER THE LOW BROILER FOR 5 MINUTES TO CRISP UP THE SKIN! OTHERWISE, REMOVE AND DISCARD THE SKIN BEFORE SERVING. SERVE WITH RICE AND TOP WITH THE SAUCE.

Tips for Cooking Delicious Seafood

- Fish, shellfish and other seafood cooks quickly and deliciously in a pressure cooker. Because it cooks so fast, pressure cooking is virtually the only method (other than pre-marinading) to infuse the flavors of the broth, butter and seasonings into the meat.

- Seafood generally has very little fat or muscle and therefore cooks very fast. Allow 2 minutes per 1" thickness of fish or pound of shellfish. Also, if you have the option, use a low pressure setting.

- Before adding the seafood or fish to the cooker, bring the liquid to a boil first. Then add the food, quickly attach the lid and bring up to pressure.

- Select pieces of fish with uniform size and thickness.

- For steaming, wrap fish in cheesecloth or parchment paper before pressure cooking. Place on a rack above the liquid for the best results.

- Use liquid amounts as outlined in the Cooking Time Charts.

- Quick-release pressure Manually unless otherwise noted in the recipe.

Fish & Seafood

Fish, shellfish and other seafood cooks so quickly that pressure cooking is virtually the only method to infuse the flavors of the broth, butter and seasonings into the meat while cooking!

MUSSELS MARINARA

Prep Time: 5 minutes   Ready in: 18 minutes   Yield: Allow 1/2 lb of mussels per serving

INGREDIENTS
2 Tbsp Olive oil
1 medium onion; diced
½ small red pepper; diced
¼ Cup clam juice
1 28-oz. can crushed tomatoes
¼ Cup tomato paste
1 Tbsp Fresh chopped basil (or 2 tsp. Dried)
1 Tbsp Fresh chopped oregano (or 2 tsp. Dried)
1 Tbsp Fresh chopped thyme (or 2 tsp. Dried)
1 tsp Salt
pinch crushed red pepper
pinch sugar
2-3 lbs. fresh mussels; wash, inspect and use only tightly closed mussels free of cracks.

DIRECTIONS
1. Place your pressure cooker on a level surface, insert the pressure pot, and plug the unit in.
2. Set Cook Time to 5 minutes or select the preprogrammed Brown button. Press Start.
3. Add oil and when hot, add and sauté the onion and red pepper for 2-3 minutes.
4. Add the clam juice, crushed tomatoes, tomato paste, herbs and remaining seasonings.
5. Attach lid and set pressure valve to Air Tight. Press Cancel and set Cook Time for 10 minutes.
6. After cooking time has elapsed, quickly release the pressure and safely remove the lid. Stir the sauce and add the mussels.
7. Replace lid, adjust valve to Air Tight and set Cook Time to 3 minutes. When cooking time has elapsed, quickly release pressure.
8. Serve immediately with pasta and hot crusty bread.

TIP: FOR A QUICKER VERSION, ADD 1 JAR OF YOUR FAVORITE MARINARA SAUCE, 1/4 CUP CLAM JUICE AND THE MUSSELS
AND PRESS "FISH" OR SET COOK TIME TO 3 MINUTES.

SHRIMP SCAMPI

Prep Time: 10 minutes   Ready in: 5 minutes   Yield: 2-4 servings

INGREDIENTS
12-24 large shrimp; peeled and deveined
3 cloves garlic; coarsely chopped
4 Tbsp butter
1 Tbsp olive oil
2 tsp dried parsley flakes
½ tsp salt
lemon wedges
1 1/2 Cups water

DIRECTIONS
1. Place your pressure cooker on a level surface, insert the pressure pot, and plug the unit in.
2. Place a meat rack (of any height) into the bottom of the cooker. Add the water.
3. Combine the butter, oil, garlic, parsley and salt and heat in the microwave until butter is melted.
4. Place shrimp in a single layer into a shallow oven-safe glass dish or cake pan that fits into your pressure cooker. Pour butter and garlic mixture over the shrimp; toss to coat. Carefully lower the shrimp onto the top of the rack.
5. Attach lid and set pressure valve to the Air Tight position.
6. Set Cook Time for 4 minutes and press Start.
7. When cook time has elapsed, manually release pressure until the lid can be safely removed.
8. Serve Shrimp immediately with fresh lemon wedges or over pasta or rice with a little of the garlic-butter sauce!

TIP: IF YOU DO NOT HAVE A PAN THAT WILL FIT INTO YOUR PRESSURE COOKER MAKE A FOIL POUCH/BOWL.
IF YOU DO NOT HAVE A RACK, SCATTER A FEW JAR LIDS ONTO THE BOTTOM!

CLAM SAUCE WITH LINGUINE

Prep Time: 7 minutes   Ready in: 13 minutes   Yield: 4 servings

INGREDIENTS

2 Tbsp good olive oil
3 cloves garlic, minced
¾ Cup chopped fresh basil
1 8-oz. bottle clam juice
½ tsp Crushed red pepper
1 29-oz. can diced tomatoes
1 8-oz. can tomato sauce
2 Cups hot water
1 lb. box linguine
3 6.5-oz. cans chopped clams
grated Parmesan cheese

DIRECTIONS

1. Open the cans of clams and drain the liquid into a measuring cup together with the tomato sauce and water.
2. Mince the garlic, coarsely chop the basil and have everything else handy before starting.
3. Place your pressure cooker on a level surface, insert the pressure pot, and plug the unit in.
4. Set Cook Time to 6 minutes or press the preprogrammed Vegetable button and adjust from there. Press Start.
5. Add olive oil to pan and when hot, add garlic. Stiring constantly to prevent over-browning, sauté about 1 minute.
6. Add basil and quickly saute until the leaves begin to wilt. Add the crushed red pepper and stir in the tomato/water mixture.
7. Break the linguine noodles in half and add to the pot. Stir well to separate noodles, for about 1 minute.
8. Attach lid and set the pressure valve to Air Tight (closed).
9. When cooking time has elapsed, quickly release steam. Carefully remove the lid and gently stir to separate noodles.
10. Add clams, cover with glass lid (or use pressure lid with valve set to exhaust) and simmer for 1 minute.
11. Toss together and serve with Parmesan cheese and garlic bread.

SHRIMP CREOLE

Prep Time: 5 minutes   Ready in: 10 minutes   Yield: 2-4 servings

INGREDIENTS
½ cup flour
½ cup corn oil
1 cups onions; chopped
½ cup celery; chopped
¼ cup bell pepper; chopped
1 cloves garlic; chopped
1 14.5-oz. Can diced tomatoes
1 small can tomato paste
1 ½ teaspoon salt
pinch red pepper flakes; more if a spicier dish is desired
¼ teaspoon black pepper
3 cups water
1 ½ pounds medium sized raw shrimp; peeled and deveined
1 tablespoon chopped parsley

DIRECTIONS
1. Prep all of the veggies and shrimp before starting this recipe.
2. Place your pressure cooker on a level surface, insert the pressure pot, and plug the unit in.
3. Set Cook Time for 5 minutes or press the preprogrammed Fish button and adjust time if necessary.
4. Add oil to pan and when hot, make a roux by browning the flour in the oil over low heat. Add the onions, celery, pepper and garlic and cook stir in the until soft. Add tomatoes, tomato paste, salt and the red and black pepper.
5. Mix well, cook for about 2-3 minutes and then add the 3 cups water. .
6. Stir in the shrimp. Attach the lid and turn the exhaust valve to the Air Tight (closed) position.
7. When cooking time has elapsed, manually release the pressure. Carefully open the lid.
8. Stir the mixture well and serve over rice Top with chopped fresh parsley and onion 5 minutes before serving.

TERIYAKI MAHI WITH RICE

Prep Time: 5 minutes   Ready in: 20 minutes   Yield: 2-4 servings

INGREDIENTS
2-4 8-oz Mahi fillets without skin
1/4 Cup Teriyaki Sauce
2 Tbsp sesame seeds (optional)
2 Tbsp vegetable oil
3 1/2 Cups Chicken Broth
1/2 tsp garlic salt
1 Cup pineapple tidbits; canned, frozen or fresh
2 Cups long grain white rice

DIRECTIONS
1. Wash the Mahi and put into a zip-top baggie with the Teriyaki sauce. Place in refrigerator for 1 hour.
2. When the hour is up, remove the fish to a plate. Discard remaining Teriyaki and baggie.
3. Sprinkle the sesame seeds evenly on one side only of the fish fillets; about 1 tsp per fillet.
1. Place your pressure cooker on a level surface, insert the pressure pot, and plug the unit in.
2. Set Cook Time for 12 minutes or press the preprogrammed Rice button. Press Start.
3. Add oil to the pot. When hot, carefully place the fish fillets, seed side down, into the pan. Let sear 1-2 minutes before turning over and transferring back to a plate.
4. Add the rice to the pan along with the chicken broth and garlic salt. Stir until the rice begins to boil. Stir in the pineapple and carefully lay the fish fillets into the rice, seed side up.
5. Attach lid and set pressure valve to the Air Tight position.
6. When cook time has elapsed, manually release pressure until the lid can be safely removed.
7. Check to be sure the rice is tender. If not, remove the fish to a plate, attach lid to the pressure cooker cook on Keep Warm until rice is ready. Serve Mahi with the rice.

TIP - SERVE THIS DISH WITH FRESH FRUIT SALSA FOR ADDED FLAVOR AND BEAUTY!

MOCK PAELLA

Prep Time: 15 minutes   Ready in: 20 minutes   Yield: 8 servings

INGREDIENTS
2 Tbsp olive oil
½ lb. boneless, skinless chicken breast; cut into small cubes
8 oz. Salami or Pepperoni; cut into small cubes
1 med. Onion; chopped
2 cloves garlic; chopped
1 10-oz. package Vigo yellow rice
1 14.5-oz. can petite diced tomatoes
2 Cups chicken broth
1 lb. 16-20 count shrimp; peeled and deveined
12 little neck clams or mussels; scrubbed and bearded (optional)
3 small bay leaves

DIRECTIONS
1. Place your pressure cooker on a level surface, insert the pressure pot, and plug the unit in.
2. Set Cook Time to 5 minutes or select the preprogrammed Brown button. Press Start.
3. Add the olive oil and when hot, add the chicken, salami and onion. Cook, stirring often for about 5 minutes. Add the garlic and continue cooking another minute.
4. Add the rice, tomatoes and broth; stir well. Gently stir in the shrimp, the clams or mussels if desired and the bay leaves.
5. Attach the lid and set the valve to Air Tight (closed). Press Cancel and then select the preprogrammed Rice button or set Cook Time for 12 minutes.
6. When cooking time has elapsed, unplug the machine and let sit 5 minutes before manually releasing the remaining pressure. Carefully remove lid.
7. Serve immediately with crusty bread and offer Tabasco Sauce on the side.

CAJUN CRAWFISH BOIL

Prep Time: 5 minutes   Ready in: 20 minutes   Yield: 8 servings

INGREDIENTS
8-10 small red potatoes
4 Cups hot water
1 tsp salt
8 ears of corn; halved
1 stick butter
1 lb. large, raw, shell-on or off, shrimp
1 lb. mussels or clams
1 lb. crayfish; frozen, raw or cooked, shelled or not
2 Tbsp crab or shrimp boil seasoning

DIRECTIONS
1. Place your pressure cooker on a level surface, insert the pressure pot, and plug the unit in.
2. Set cooking time to 6 minutes and press Start.
3. Add 4 cups hot water, salt and the potatoes. Attach lid and set valve to Air Tight.
4. When time has elapsed, switch off the keep warm feature and exhaust the pressure. Re set the cooking time to 6 minutes and press Start.
5. Add the corn and the butter; Attach lid and set valve to Air Tight.
6. When time has elapsed, switch off the keep warm feature and exhaust the pressure. Reset cooking time to 3 minutes and press start.
7. Add the seafood and seasoning; stir well. Attach lid and set valve to Air Tight.
8. When time has elapsed, switch off the keep warm feature and let rest 5 minutes before Manually releasing the pressure.

TIP: BASE YOUR QUANTITIES ON THE SIZE OF YOUR PRESSURE COOKER!
USE WHATEVER COMBO OF SEAFOOD THAT YOU PREFER,
BUT IF YOU ADD FISH OR LOBSTER TAILS PUT THEM IN WITH THE CORN FOR THE ADDED COOK TIME!

Mediterranean Salmon

Prep Time: 5 minutes   Ready in: 10 minutes   Yield: 2-4 servings

INGREDIENTS
1 pound salmon fillet, washed
1 halved lemon
1/2 teaspoon dried oregano
1/2 teaspoon dried parsley
1 medium tomato, seeded and chopped
8 small black olives, pitted and sliced
2 teaspoons capers
2 tablespoons white wine
1 1/2 cups water
1 Cup cooked white rice per serving.

DIRECTIONS
1. Place the salmon on a large square of aluminum foil. Squeeze the lemon over the fillet and top with the next 6 ingredients. Pinch the foil together to form a tight packet that seals in the fish.
2. Place your pressure cooker on a level surface, insert the pressure pot, and plug the unit in.
3. Set Cook Time for 7 minutes or press the preprogrammed Fish button and adjust time if necessary.
4. Add the water to the bottom of the pressure cooker pot and place rack into the cooker (if available). Sit the fish onto the rack.
5. Attach the lid and turn the exhaust valve to the Air Tight (closed) position.
6. When cooking time has elapsed, manually release the pressure. Carefully open the lid.
7. Remove steamer basket and rack. Open foil pouch and serve fish with the white rice.

T

THIS RECIPE CAN BE MADE WITH JUST ABOUT ANY GOOD WILD-CAUGHT FISH SO EXPERIMENT WITH YOUR FAVORITE!

TV Tidbit - You may have seen this recipe made on TV by placing the fish on a taller rack and cooking the rice underneath. You can absolutley do that but increase the thickness of the fish to at least 1" to account for the increased cooktime needed by the rice; increase cooktime to 12 minutes.

Sweet Bourbon Salmon

Prep Time: 5 minutes   Ready in: 10 minutes   Yield: 2-4 servings

INGREDIENTS
1/4 Cup pineapple juice
1/4 tsp cracked black pepper
2 Tbsp soy sauce
1/8 tsp garlic powder
2 Tbsp brown sugar
1/2 Cup vegetable oil
1 Tbsp Kentucky bourbon
2-4 8-oz salmon fillets without skin
2 Tbsp snipped fresh chives
1 1/2 Cups water

DIRECTIONS
1. Place your pressure cooker on a level surface, insert the pressure pot, and plug the unit in.
2. Place a meat rack (of any height) into the bottom of the cooker. Add the water.
3. Combine pineapple juice, soy sauce, brown sugar, bourbon, pepper and garlic powder in bowl. Stir to dissolve the sugar then add the oil.
4. Put salmon fillets into a shallow oven-safe glass dish or cake pan that fits into your pressure cooker. Pour bourbon marinade over the fish. Carefully lower the fish onto the top of the rack.
5. Attach lid and set pressure valve to the Air Tight position.
6. Set Cook Time for 5 minutes for medium and 7 minutes for medium well and press Start.
7. When cook time has elapsed, manually release pressure until the lid can be safely removed.
8. Serve Salmon with a little sauce and top with fresh chives.

**TIP: IF YOU DO NOT HAVE A PAN THAT WILL FIT INTO YOUR PRESSURE COOKER MAKE A FOIL POUCH/BOWL.
IF YOU DO NOT HAVE A RACK, SCATTER A FEW JAR LIDS ONTO THE BOTTOM!**

JUMBO MAINE LOBSTERS

Prep Time: 3 minutes   Ready in: 10 minutes   Yield: allow 1/3-1/2 lb. per serving

INGREDIENTS
2-6 whole maine lobsters
1 Tbsp vegetable oil
1 Cup celery; cut into 2" stalks
1 Cup onion; cut into quarters
1 Cup water
3 Bay leaves
1 Tbsp lemon juice
Butter

DIRECTIONS
1. Place your pressure cooker on a level surface, insert the pressure pot, and plug the unit in.
2. Set the Cook Time for 12 minutes or select and adjust the preprogrammed Seafood button; press Start.
3. Add the oil to the pot and when hot, add the celery, onion water, bay leaves and lemon juice.
4. Place the lobsters into the pot in a tic-tac-toe pattern.
5. Attach the lid and turn the pressure valve to Air Tight.
6. When the cooking time has elapsed, place a damp paper towel loosely over the exhaust valve and release the pressure.
7. Leave the lobsters in the pot until ready to serve; up to 15 minutes.
8. Serve with drawn butter.

TV Tidbit: When Kelly opened the lid of the Elite 10qt PC to reveal 6 jumbo lobsters it was a thing of beauty! Fortunately for your budget, you will probably never need to cook more than 4 at a time so the 8 qt will be perfect too!

PEEL AND EAT SHRIMP

Prep Time: 3 minutes   Ready in: 7 minutes   Yield: allow 1/3-1/2 lb. per serving

INGREDIENTS
2 lb. medium raw, shell-on, head off shrimp, washed
1 bottle of your favorite beer
2 Tbsp Old Bay seasoning

DIRECTIONS
1. Place your pressure cooker on a level surface, insert the pressure pot, and plug the unit in.
2. Set the Cook Time for 3 minutes or select the preprogrammed Seafood button; press Start.
3. Pour the beer into the pot and when hot, add the shrimp and top with the Old Bay seasoning.
4. Attach the lid and turn the pressure valve to Air Tight.
5. When the cooking time has elapsed, place a damp paper towel loosely over the exhaust valve and release the pressure.
6. Drain the shrimp and serve hot. Sprinkle a little more Old Bay on the shrimp if desired.

TIP: TO SERVE A CROWD, THIS RECIPE MAY BE EXPANDED UP TO 10 POUNDS. THE RULE OF THUMB IS 1 BOTTLE OF BEER PER 5 POUNDS OF SHRIMP AND 1 TBS. OF OLD BAY SEASONING PER POUND OF SHRIMP.
IF YOU COOK MORE THAN 5 POUNDS, INCREASE THE TIME TO 5 MINUTES.

CRAB FEAST

Prep Time: 5 minutes   Ready in: 10 minutes   Yield: 1 per servings

INGREDIENTS
2 snow crab clusters per serving; the 8 quart cooker can easily accommodate 8-10 clusters
2 Cups hot water
1 tsp salt
1 stick butter
2 Tbsp crab or shrimp boil seasoning
1/2 stick butter

DIRECTIONS
1. Place your pressure cooker on a level surface, insert the pressure pot, and plug the unit in.
2. Set cooking time to 5 minutes and press Start.
3. Add 2 cups hot water, salt and the crabs. Attach lid and set valve to Air Tight.
4. When time has elapsed, switch off the Keep Warm feature and exhaust the pressure.
5. Transfer the crab legs to a platter and top with a little broth from the bottom of the pan.
6. Or...Serve immediately straight from the pot to keep them warm between servings!

Serve with drawn butter and lots of napkins!

TIPS FOR COOKING PASTA

Most manufacturers make disclaimers warning against pressure cooking pasta. This is based on the fear that starches from the pasta may clog the exhaust regulator and pose a safety hazard. This is a very valid point and extra care should be taken when cooking pastas and rices.

By following the tips below you CAN cook pasta... safely, quickly and deliciously!

- Make sure ingredients never exceed half the capacity of the cooker.

- Always add 2 Tablespoons oil to the liquid to minimize the starchy foam.

- Release steam using the Natural Release or Cold Water Method only.

- Wash the lid, gasket and exhaust valve thoroughly after cooking pasta. Every time, no exceptions! If there is a metal cap covering the valve inside the lid, pop it off and wash it too! Just don't put a toothpick in the valve as it may break off.

Pasta, Rice, Beans & Grains

Tips and Time Charts for Cooking Rice and Grains

Rinsing

- Rinsing the rice and grains is an important step that should not be skipped! Always rinse grains and rice under lukewarm water before cooking. It will help remove the starch that make the rice sticky and clumpy as well as any dirt and debris left behind by the packaging process.

Soaking

- Although rice and most grains do not require soaking, larger grains such as wheat berries and pearl barley must be soaked before cooking.
- It is not necessary to soak overnight; pressure soak instead! Your whole grains will cook MUCH faster!
- Pour 4 cups water and 1 cup grains into the pressure cooker. Do not add salt to the water during the soaking process as it will inhibit hydration.
- Bring to pressure and cook 2 minutes.
- Release pressure naturally.
- Drain the grains and cook as directed.

Cooking

- Most electric pressure cookers will have a preset rice function or recipes specific to that model; be sure to follow the manufactures directions.
- Allow 2 ¼ cups water for each cup of rice along with 1 teaspoon salt and 1 Tablespoon oil.
- Do NOT omit oil! It reduces foaming and clogging.
- Never fill the cooker more than halfway with rice or grains.
- Release steam using the Natural Release or Cold Water Method only.
- Remove the rice from the pan immediately to prevent over-cooking or scorching.
- Wash the lid, gasket and exhaust valve thoroughly after cooking rice and grains.

IF THE PRESSURE COOKER IS HISSING, OR IF ANY STEAM IS ESCAPING, IT IS **NOT** UNDER FULL PRESSURE. JIGGLE THE EXHAUST VALVE UNTIL IT IS SILENT WITH NO STEAM!

Cooking Time Chart for Rice

Rice (1 Cup)	MINIMUM LIQUID	MIN COOK TIME	RELEASE METHOD
Arborio Rice	2 1/2 Cups	24-25 min	Quick or Natural
Brown Rice, long grain	2 Cup	24-25 min	Natural
Brown Rice, short grain	2 Cup	28-29 min	Natural
White Rice, long grain;	1 2/3 Cup	15 min	Quick or Natural
Basmati and Jasmine	1 2/3 Cups	15 min	Natural
White Rice, short grain	2 1/2 Cups	18 min	Natural
Rice, Wild	4 Cups	35 min	Natural

Cooking Time Chart for Grains

Grain (1 Cup)	MINIMUM LIQUID	MIN COOK TIME	RELEASE METHOD
Barley, Pearl	4 1/2 Cups	18-20 min	Natural
Barley, Whole	3 Cups	20 min	Natural
Bulgur, Cracked Wheat	3 Cups	8-10 min	Natural
Corn, Grits & Polenta	3 1/2 Cups	10	Quick
Couscous	2 Cups	3 min	Quick
Oats, Rolled	4 Cups	6 min	Natural
Oats, Steel Cut, Scotch, Irish, Whole	4 Cups	11 min	Natural
Quinoa	2 Cups	6 min	

BEANS & LEGUME COOKING TIME CHART

BEAN TYPE	SOAKED COOK TIME MINUTES	UNSOAKED COOK TIME MINUTES	RELEASE METHOD
Adzuki (aka red cow pea, red chori)	10	20	Natural
Beans, black	16-18	25	Natural
Beans, cannellini (white kidney)	15	35	Natural
Beans, chickpeas (garbanzo or kabu-li)	16	35	Natural
Beans, great northern	15	30	Natural
Beans, lima baby	6	15	Natural
Beans, lima large	7	18	Natural
Beans, navy or white haricot	17	34-40	Natural
Beans, pinto	14	33-35	Natural
Beans, kidney (red)	15	35	Natural
Beans, soy (tan)	10-12	30-35	Natural
Beans, soy (black)	20-23	35-40	Natural
Gandules (pigeon peas)	16-18	25	Natural
Lentils, French green	-	12	Quick
Lentils, green, mini (brown)	-	10	Quick
Lentils, red or yellow split	-	8	Quick
Peas, split, green or yellow	-	10	Natural
Peas, dried black-eyed	-	12	Natural

Tips for Cooking Beans and Lentils

Most dried beans will require soaking before cooking. However, it is a much quicker process than the conventional overnight method! Just remember these 2 tips:
- Do not add salt during the soaking process or it will toughen the beans.
- Do not soak lentils or split peas.

Pressure Cooker Soaking Directions
1. Pour 4 cups water and 1 cup dried beans or peas into the pressure cooker.
2. Bring to pressure and cook 5 minutes.
3. Release pressure using the cold water method.
4. Drain the beans and cook as directed.

General Cooking Directions
- Use 3 cups liquid for every 1 cup of soaked beans.
- Always add 1 Tablespoon oil to the cooking water.
- Use the Natural Release Method to release the steam after cooking. Do not quick release!
- Wash the lid, gasket and exhaust valve throughly before storing.

NOTE: DISCARDING THE SOAKING WATER AND REPLACING WITH FRESH LIQUID WILL CUT DOWN ON THE GAS-PRODUCING QUALITY OF THE BEANS. YOU MAY ALSO WANT TO ADD A PRODUCT CALLED BEANO® TO FURTHER REDUCE STOMACH-UPSETTING GASSES.

HARVEST GRAIN PILAF

Prep Time: 11 minutes   Ready in: 33 minutes   Yield: 4-6 servings

INGREDIENTS
1 1/2 Tbsp butter
1 Cup thinly sliced Leek
1/2 Cup thinly sliced celery
2 1/2 Cups water
1 1/2 Cups Chicken Broth
1/2 Cup long grained brown rice
1/2 Cup uncooked pearl barley
1/4 Cup uncooked bulgur
1/2 Cup dried Cranberries or Raisins
1/4 Cup fresh parsley; chopped
1/4 tsp black pepper
1 tsp sugar
1/2 Cup toasted almond slices or other nut

DIRECTIONS
1. Place your pressure cooker on a level surface, insert the pressure pot, and plug the unit in.
2. Set Cook Time for 28 minutes or select the preprogrammed Brown Rice Button. Press Start.
3. Add the butter to the pan and when melted, add the leeks and the celery. Cook 2-3 minutes. Stir in the water, broth, brown rice and barley.
4. Attach and lock the lid of your pressure cooker; set the pressure control to "air tight" or closed.
5. When cooking time has elapsed, manually release the pressure and carefully open the lid.
6. Stir the Cranberries or Raisins, the bulgur and the sugar into the mixture. Reattach the lid and set pressure valve to Air Tight.
7. Set Cook Time for 4 minutes and press Start.
8. Meanwhile, toast 1/2 Cup of almond slices or slivers, chopped pecans or nuts in a 350 oven for 5 minutes.
9. When pressure cooking time has elapsed, wait 5 minutes before manually releasing the pressure.
10. Serve hot topped with the toasted nuts, fresh parsley and fresh ground black pepper.

SIMPLE BROWN RICE

Prep Time: 3 minutes   Ready in: 33 minutes   Yield: 4-6 servings

INGREDIENTS
1 1/2 Cup long grained brown rice
1 1/2 Tbsp butter
3 Cups water
1 Tbsp Better than Bouillon® Chicken Base

DIRECTIONS
1. Place your pressure cooker on a level surface, insert the pressure pot, and plug the unit in.
2. Set Cook Time for 28 minutes or select the preprogrammed Brown Rice Button. Press Start.
3. Add the butter to the pan and when melted, add the rice. Stir until the rice is coated with the butter.
4. Mix the bouillon into the water and microwave for 3 minutes or until the bouillon dissolves. Pour into the rice.
5. Stir the rice well. Once the mixture begins to bubble, stir again.
6. Attach and lock the lid of your pressure cooker; set the pressure control to "air tight" or closed.
7. When cooking time has elapsed, manually release the pressure by opening the pressure control valve to exhaust.
8. Once the pressure has been released, carefully open the lid and stir.

TIP: THIS RECIPE CAN BE EASILY DOUBLED, TRIPLED OR QUADRUPLED DEPENDING ON THE SIZE OF YOUR PRESSURE COOKER. JUST BE SURE TO INCREASE THE BUTTER AND WATER ACCORDINGLY.

QUINOA W/ LEMON AND CORN

Prep Time: 15 minutes   Ready in: 15 minutes   Yield: 8-10 servings

INGREDIENTS
4 ears of corn; husk and silk removed
4 Cup water
2 Cups quinoa; white, red or mixed
4 scallions; whites and one inch of the green thinly sliced
1/2 Cup fresh mint; chopped
1/2 Cup orange bell pepper; chopped
Zest of 2 lemons
Juice of 2 lemons
1 tsp salt
1/4 tsp pepper
1/2 Tbsp honey
1/4 Cup extra virgin olive oil

DIRECTIONS
1. Place your pressure cooker on a level surface, insert the pressure pot, and plug the unit in.
2. Place corn into pot and add 1 Cup of water.
3. Attach and lock the lid of your pressure cooker and set the pressure control to "air tight" or closed.
4. Set cook time for 3 minutes; press Start. When cooking time has elapsed, manually release the pressure.
5. Carefully open the lid and transfer corn, with thongs, to a cutting board. When cool enough to handle, cut kernels off cobs with heavy knife or mandolin.
6. Meanwhile, in a large bowl, whisk together the lemon zest and juice, salt, pepper and honey. Continue whisking while slowly drizzling in the olive oil.
7. Remove pressure pot. Wash, dry and return the pot to the cooker.
8. Place quinoa into a sieve and wash three times or until water runs clear. Place couscous into pressure pot and stir in the remaining 3 Cups of water.
9. Attach and lock the lid of your pressure cooker and set the pressure control to "air tight" or closed.
10. Set cook time for 1 minute; press Start. When cooking time has elapsed, let pressure release naturally.
11. Prepare the mint, bell peppers and scallions as directed.
12. Carefully open the lid of your pressure cooker and transfer the couscous into the bowl containing your lemon mixture; mix well.
13. Gently stir in the scallions, peppers and mint; serve immediately.

132

Quinoa w/ Toasted Pine Nuts

Prep Time: 15 minutes   Ready in: 15 minutes   Yield: 8-10 servings

INGREDIENTS

2 Cups quinoa; white, red or mixed
2 tsp olive oil
6-7 medium scallions
1 Tbsp garlic cloves; minced
2 1/2 Cups chicken broth
1/2 tsp salt
1/2 tsp fresh ground black pepper
1/2 Cup pine nuts
1/2 Cup fresh basil leaves; sliced into ribbons

DIRECTIONS

1. Place your pressure cooker on a level surface, insert the pressure pot, and plug the unit in.
2. Place quinoa into a sieve and wash three times or until water runs clear; set aside.
3. Prepare scallions by slicing the white and light green from 4 scallions into thin rings. Cut the light greens from 2 onions into long, thin lenghtwise pieces.
4. Set Cook Time to 1 minute, press Start.
5. Add oil to the pot and when hot add the sliced scallion rings; stir quickly.
6. Add the garlic and saute just 1 minute.
7. Stir in the quinoa and the chicken broth.
8. Attach and lock the lid of your pressure cooker and set the pressure control to "Air Tight" or closed.
9. When cooking time has elapsed, let pressure release naturally.
10. Prepare the basil and scallion greens as directed. Place the pine nuts in a hot pan on the stove and cook 3 minutes or until beginning to brown. You may also brown the nuts in the oven if you prefer.
11. Carefully open the lid of your pressure cooker.
12. Gently stir in the basil, salt and pepper.
13. Serve in bowls topped with scallion strips and toasted pine nuts.

BLACK BEANS

Prep Time: 15 minutes   Ready in: 90 minutes   Yield: 8-10 servings

INGREDIENTS
1 pound black beans
5 Cups water
2 tablespoons olive oil
1 large yellow onion; chopped
1 green pepper; chop half
2 cloves garlic; minced
6 Cups water
1 large smoked ham hock
2 bay leaves
½ tsp salt
½ tsp cumin
1/2 tsp paprika

DIRECTIONS

1. Place your pressure cooker on a level surface, insert the pressure pot, and plug the unit in.
2. Wash and sort through the beans; pick out and discard any small stones. Place into the pressure pan and cover by 2 inches with cold water; about 5 Cups for an 8 qt pressure cooker. Add 1/2 of the green pepper; seeds and membrane removed, left intactt.
3. Attach and lock the lid and set the pressure control to Air Tight or closed.
4. Set cook time for 5 minutes; press Start. When cooking time has elapsed, press Cancel to turn off the Keep Warm setting and let pressure release naturally.
5. Carefully open the lid. Remove and discard green pepper. Carefully pour the beans through a colander to drain. Rinse the beans well, drain and set aside.
6. Wash, dry and replace the pressure pot into the cooker base. Set Cook Time for 40 minutes or press the preprogrammed Bean button. Add oil and, when hot, add the onion, pepper and garlic, reduce heat to medium and sauté for 3-4 minutes until the onion is soft but not brown.
7. Add the 6 cups of water, the ham hock, bay leaves, salt, cumin and paprika. Add the beans and bring to a boil. Attach the lid and set the regulator to Air Tight.
8. When cooking time has elapsed, let pressure release naturally and remove the lid.
9. Discard the ham hock and bay leaves. Using a slotted spoon, scoop out 1 cup of beans and mash them. Return the mashed beans to the pot and stir well. Cook uncovered over Keep Warm another 15 minutes.
10. Serve alone or over cooked white rice; top with chopped onion.

Cowboy Beans

Prep Time: 10 minutes   Ready in: 25 minutes   Yield: 8-10 servings

INGREDIENTS
2 Tbsp vegetable oil
1 Cup onion; coarsely chopped
1 Cup green bell pepper; coarsely chopped
1 lb. lean ground beef
1 27-oz can light red kidney beans; drained
1 27-oz can dark red kidney beans; drained
2 16-oz cans chili beans; undrained
1 6-oz can tomato paste
1 Cup brown sugar
2 tsp dried mustard
1 tsp chili powder
2 tsp Worcestershire sauce
2 Cups water

DIRECTIONS
1. Place your pressure cooker on a level surface, insert the pressure pot, and plug the unit in. Set the Cook Time to 9 minutes and press Start.
2. Add hamburger and cook until browned; stirring often. Drain and set aside.
3. Add oil, onions and peppers and cook for about 2 minutes or until onion is starting to soften but is not yet browned.
4. Add the brown sugar, tomato paste, dried mustard, chili powder, Worcestershire sauce and water. Gently stir until the mixture is bubbly and well mixed.
5. Stir in the ground beef and the beans.
6. Attach and Close lid and set exhaust valve to "Airtight" or closed.
7. When cooking time has elapsed, unplug pressure cooker and let the pressure release naturally.
8. Serve as-is or finish the dish off by transferring to a baking dish, sprinkling lightly with brown sugar and cooking in a 350 oven 15-20 minutes for a "baked bean" flavor.

TIP: THIS CAN EASILY BE MADE FROM DRIED BEANS BY FOLLOWING THE SOAK AND COOK TIME ON THE CHARTS
AND THEN ADDING TO THE RECIPE AS ABOVE.

QUICK RED BEANS & RICE
Prep Time: 10 minutes   Ready in: 20 minutes   Yield: 6-8 servings

INGREDIENTS
2 Tbsp Olive oil
3 Tbsp butter
1 Cup onion; coarsely chopped
1 Cup green bell pepper; coarsely chopped
½ lb. kielbasa sausage sliced thin; optional
1 27-oz can light red kidney beans; drained
2 Cups converted rice
1 Tbsp Creole seasoning; or more to taste
4 ¾ Cups hot water

DIRECTIONS
1. Place your pressure cooker on a level surface, insert the pressure pot, and plug the unit in. Set the Cook Time to 9 minutes and press Start.
2. Add oil, butter, onions and peppers; add ½ lb. sliced kielbasa sausage if desired.
3. Cook for about 2 minutes or until onion is starting to soften but is not yet browned.
4. Add the beans, rice and seasoning and stir well.
5. Add the water and stir again.
6. Attach and Close lid and set exhaust valve to "Airtight" or closed.
7. When cooking time has elapsed, unplug pressure cooker and let sit 5 minutes and then manually release the pressure. You may also allow pressure to release naturally.

TIP: THIS CAN EASILY BE MADE FROM DRIED KIDNEY BEANS BY FOLLOWING THE SOAK AND COOK TIME ON THE CHARTS AND THEN ADDING TO THE RECIPE AS ABOVE.

Chicken & Vegetable Risotto

Prep Time: 20 minutes   Ready in: 90 min with raw; 40 min for cooked   Yield: 6-8 servings

INGREDIENTS
3-4 lb. Whole Fryer Chicken
2 Tbsp Olive Oil
1 Tbsp Butter
1 Medium Onion (coarsely chopped)
6 Cups canned chicken broth
1 ¼ Cup chopped celery
1 ¼ Cup chopped carrots
½ lb. Sliced mushrooms
¼ Cup chopped parsley
2 tsp kosher salt
1 tsp Ground black pepper
1 ¾ Cup risotto
¾ Cup Parmesan cheese

DIRECTIONS
1. Wash, pat dry, lightly salt and pepper chicken inside and out; set aside.
2. Place your pressure cooker on a level surface, insert the pressure pot, and plug the unit in.
3. Set the Cook Time to 10 minutes and press Start. Add the olive oil and butter and when hot add the onion and lightly brown. Add chicken broth and scrape the bottom of the pan with a rubber or wooden spoon. Place the chicken into the pot. Attach lid and set pressure to airtight.
4. Press the Cancel and then set Cook Time to 45 minutes. When unit turns to keep warm, turn it off and let stand 15 minutes. Release the remaining pressure manually or by allowing it to naturally cool.
5. Using a skimmer spoon or other long handled utensil, carefully remove the chicken and allow it to cool until you can easily handle it. Remove the bones and skin from the chicken and discard. Strain the broth through a sieve to remove and unsavory bits.
6. Cut chicken into bite size pieces and return to the broth along with the remaining ingredients. Replace pressure lid and set time for 13 minutes. When cooking time has elapsed, unplug pressure cooker and let sit until no pressure remains. Carefully open the lid of your pressure cooker and gently stir in the Parmesan cheese. If the risotto is not creamy enough, add warm water or broth, 1/4 Cup at a time, until it reaches the perfect consistency. Serve immediately topped with shaved Parmesan cheese and a crisp green salad on the side.

TIP: COOK QUICKER BY USING A ROTISSERIE CHICKEN FROM YOUR LOCAL GROCERY OR DELI!
CHANGE COOK TIME TO 10 MINUTES AND THEN CONTINUE AS DIRECTED ABOVE.

CHICK PEAS AND SPINACH

Prep Time: 10 minutes   Ready in: 75 minutes   Yield: 8-10 servings

INGREDIENTS

1 pound dried chick peas (garbonza beans)
2 tablespoons olive oil
1 medium yellow onion; finely chopped
1 green pepper; finely chopped
1/4 tsp dried minced garlic
1 tsp paprika
½ tsp salt
2 Cups Chicken or Vegetable Broth
1 Cup water plus 2 more
2 Cups frozen spinach; thawed and squeezed dry

DIRECTIONS

1. Place your pressure cooker on a level surface, insert the pressure pot, and plug the unit in.
2. Wash and sort through the beans; pick out and discard any small stones. Set aside.
3. Set Cook Time for 45 minutes or press the preprogrammed Bean button.
4. Add oil and, when hot, add the onion and pepper. Cook about 2-3 minutes and then stir in the chicken broth, paprika, minced garlic, salt and the rinsed chick peas.
5. Attach the lid and set the regulator to Air Tight.
6. When cooking time has elapsed, let pressure release naturally and remove the lid.
7. Stir in the thawed spinach and the fire roasted peppers.
8. Reset Cook Time for 12 minutes or press the Rice button. Reattach lid and set exhaust valve to Air Tight.
9. When cook time has elapsed, let sit 10 minutes before releasing the pressure. Serve in a bowl or drain and use as a topping on chips and pita wedges.

Macaroni & Cheese
Prep Time: 5 minutes   Ready in: 25 minutes   Yield: 8-10 servings

INGREDIENTS
1 Tbs. olive oil
3 Tbs. butter
1 lb. large elbow macaroni
1 lb Velveeta Cheese; cut into large cubes
2 cups shredded Colby jack or mild cheddar cheese
½ tsp. dry mustard
½ tsp salt
½ tsp paprika
4 Cups hot water
1/2 Cup milk

DIRECTIONS
1. Place your pressure cooker on a level surface, insert the pressure pot, and plug the unit in. Set the Cook Time to 10 minutes or select the preprogrammed Rice button and adjust the time to 10 minutes.
2. Add the butter and oil to the pot. When it starts to melt, add the Velveeta cheese cubes and stir well as it begins to melt. Don't let the cheese brown!
3. Stir in the seasonings, water and macaroni.
4. Attach and lid and set exhaust valve to Air Tight. Press Cancel to stop the timer and then select Rice; press Start.
5. When cooking time has elapsed, press Cancel and wait 2-3 minutes before manually releasing the pressure.
6. Carefully open the lid and stir gently but well. Add more milk to make it creamier if desired.
7. Add the shredded cheese to the top. Cover with a glass lid or the pressure lid leaving the valve on Exhaust.
8. Serve once the cheese has melted.

TV Tidbit - Mac 'n Cheese has quickly become one of the most requested demo recipes ever! Although I don't recommend cooking more than 2 pounds of pasta at one time, you may want to add 1/4 Cup chopped jalepeno peppers and 1 small jar of chopped pimento like we do on TV. It really peps up the color and flavor!

Lasagna

Prep Time: 10 min   Ready in: 30 min   Yield: 4-6 servings

INGREDIENTS

1 ½ lbs lean ground beef
1 Tbsp olive oil
1 medium onion; finely chopped
32 oz ricotta cheese; part skim
2 large eggs
2 tsp basil leaves; dried
2 tsp oregano leaves; dried
2 tsp garlic salt
1 Tbsp parsley flakes; dried
1 26 oz jar spaghetti sauce; use your favorite!
1 1/2 Cups crushed tomatoes
32 oz ricotta cheese; part skim
1 large egg
3 Cups mozzarella cheese; shredded
1 Cup Parmesan cheese; grated
1 8 oz pkg. No-cook lasagna noodles; use 10 noodles in all.

DIRECTIONS

1. Place your pressure cooker on a level surface, insert the pressure pot, and plug the unit in. Select the preprogrammed Meat button or set the Cook Time to 12 minutes; press Start.
2. Add the oil to the pan and when hot, add ground beef. Cook 5 minutes turning and stirring often. Add the onions and peppers and cook another minute. Add the jar of spaghetti sauce, 1 Cup crushed tomatoes and 1 tsp each basil, oregano and garlic salt. Stir well. Attach and Close lid and set exhaust valve to Air Tight.
3. While sauce is cooking, combine in a medium mixing bowl, the ricotta cheese, the parmasan cheese, 1 Cup shredded mozzarella, the egg, 1 tsp each of garlic salt, basil, oregano and parsley.
4. When cooking time has elapsed, manually exhaout the pressure and carefully open the lid. Very carefully pour the hot sauce into a bowl or large measuring cup. Place pot back into the base.
5. Fill the bottom of the cooker with 3/4 Cup crushed tomatoes. Layer the bottom with the noodles. I can usually only fit 2 in the bottom and then I break a noodle into 4 strips to fill in the gaps.
6. Cover the noodles with a quarter of the cheese. Cover the cheese with 2 ladle fulls of meat sauce, then noodles. Repeat until all layers have been used. The final layer should be noodles topped with sauce.
7. Lock the lid and set pressure valve to Air Tight. When cook time has elapsed, quick release pressure and sprinkle with remaining 1 Cup mozzarella cheese. Cover and allow to rest for 10 minutes.

TORTELLINI ALFREDO

Prep Time: 7 min   Ready in: 30 min   Yield: 4-6 servings

INGREDIENTS
3 Tbsp olive oil
½ lb mushroom slices
1/2 lb ham steak; cut into small cubes
1 tsp garlic salt
1 cup hot water
1 12-oz bag 3-cheese dried tortellini; I use Barilla brand.
2 C frozen peas,
2 15-oz jars of warmed Alfredo sauce
1-2 oz finely shredded Parmasan cheese for serving

Optional - 1 lb. medium shrimp (peeled & deveined) or 1 lb. chicken breast cut into bite-sized cubes

DIRECTIONS
1. Prep the veggies and ham before starting this recipe.
2. Place your pressure cooker on a level surface, insert the pressure pot, and plug the unit in. Select the preprogrammed Rice button or set the Cook Time to 12 minutes; press Start.
3. Add the oil to the pan and when hot, add mushrooms. Cook quickly for 2-3 minutes and then add the ham, garlic salt and pepper continue cooking to warm the ham. Add the optional shrimp or chicken.
4. Add the water, pasta, peas and jars of Alfredo sauce; stir well.
5. Attach and Close lid and set exhaust valve to Air Tight.
6. Press Cancel to stop the timer and then select Rice; press Start.
7. When cooking time has elapsed, press Cancel and wait 2 minutes before manually releasing the pressure.
8. Carefully open the lid and stir gently. If the mixture is too thick, add a little warm milk until you acheive your favortite consistancy.
9. Serve hot with fresh Parmasan cheese.

TO MAKE THIS A PROTEIN-COMPLETE MEAL, TRY IT WITH SHRIMP OR CHICKEN!
JUST ADD 1 LB PEELED AND DEVEINDED SHRIMP OR 1 LB BITE-SIZED CUBES FRESH CHICKEN BREAST IN WITH THE HAM AND CONTINUE AS DIRECTED IN THE RECIPE!

CHEESY PENNE WITH CHICKEN

Prep Time: 10 minutes   Ready in: 25 minutes   Yield: 8-10 servings

INGREDIENTS
2 Tbsp vegetable oil
1/2 Cup onion; finely chopped
1/2 lb mushrooms; sliced
1/2 Cup rotisserie or baked chicken
4 slices bacon or ham
1 tsp garlic salt
1/2 tsp coarse ground black pepper
1 lb penne pasta
2 Cups Chicken Broth
2 Cups water
8-oz cream cheese
8-oz monterey jack or sharp cheddar cheese; shredded
1/4 Cup milk

DIRECTIONS
1. Prep the veggies, meats and cheeses before starting this recipe.
2. Place your pressure cooker on a level surface, insert the pressure pot, and plug the unit in. Select the preprogrammed Rice button or set the Cook Time to 12 minutes; press Start.
3. Cook the bacon strips until brown and crispy. Drain bacon on paper towel.
4. Wash, dry and replace the pot.
5. Add oil and when hot, add onions and mushrooms. Cook quickly for 2-3 minutes and then add the chicken, garlic salt and pepper. Add water, broth and pasta; stir well.
6. Attach and Close lid and set exhaust valve to Air Tight. Press Cancel to stop the timer and then select Rice; press Start. When cooking time has elapsed, press Cancel and wait 2 minutes before manually releasing the pressure.
7. Carefully open the lid and stir well, adding the cheeses and if necessary, the milk until creamy and well blended.
8. Attach the lid but keep the exhaust valve open. Keep the PC on th Keep Warm setting. Check the pasta every minute, stirring gently, until the pasta is tender enough for your taste.

TIPS FOR PRESSURE COOKING DESSERTS & SWEETS

- Desserts that use eggs and/or are cooked over a water bath, such as cheesecakes, custards, lemon curd and puddings, turn out quite delicious in a pressure cooker.

- The timing is tricky with cheesecakes and other thick batters. Use room temperature ingredients to speed the cooking process and do not overfill the pan.

- If your cooker did not come with baking dishes, be sure to select a dish that is oven-safe and will fit into your pressure cooker with at least 1 inch to spare around the edge.

- Always seal the dish tightly with foil to keep liquid from seeping into the dessert.

- For easy insertion and removal use a sling made of aluminum foil or a steamer basket under the baking dish.

- Never place the dish directly onto the bottom of the cooker. Use a steamer basket, trivet or scatter jar lid rings to keep the dish up.

- When adapting recipes use the minimum liquid required as there will be no evaporation or boil-off in the pressure cooker.

Desserts

Not just for Meats! Desserts like cheesecakes, puddings and fruits become moist and delicious cooked in a pressure cooker!

Banana Nut Rice Pudding
Blueberry Pear Cobbler
Chocolate Cherry Gooey Cake
Cinnamon Apple Cake
Coconut Rice Pudding
Hawaiian Bread Pudding
Lemon Cheesecake
Pineapple Upside Down Cake
Poached Pears
Pumpkin Cheesecake
Stuffed Apples

Pumpkin Cheesecake

Prep Time: 15 minutes   Ready in: 4 hours   Yield: 8 servings

INGREDIENTS
1 Cup cinnamon graham cracker crumbs
1/4 Cup granulated sugar
1/2 stick butter, melted
12 oz. cream cheese, softened
1 Tbsp butter
1 tsp vanilla
3/4 Cup brown sugar, firmly packed
3/4 Cup solid-pack pumpkin
2 Tbsp cornstarch
1 tsp cinnamon
3/4 tsp nutmeg
3 large eggs
2 Cups hot water
1 pint heavy whipping cream
1/2 Cup powdered sugar
1/2 tsp cinnamon
1/4 tsp nutmeg

DIRECTIONS
1. Generously butter bottom and sides of an 6" or 8" spring form pan; or the size that will fit into your pressure cooker.
2. Sprinkle graham cracker crumbs and sugar evenly on bottom of pan; drizzle butter overall. Set pan aside.
3. In large mixing bowl, mix together cream cheese, vanilla and butter.
4. Add next 5 ingredients and continue mixing. Mix in 1 egg at a time until smooth.
5. Pour into pan up to 1/2" from the lip. If using a 6" pan, do not fill the pan more than 2/3 full; save the batter for another use or discard.
6. Cover top with wax paper and then completely cover entire pan with aluminum foil crimping top and bottom edges to seal out moisture.
7. Place your pressure cooker on a level surface, insert the pressure pot, and plug the unit in.
8. Place Rack or riser in bottom of 8 qt. pressure cooker. Add the hot water and then lower cake pan into the rack. Attach the lid and turn the pressure valve to Air Tight.
9. Set Cook Time for 50 minutes for a 6" cake or 40 minutes for an 8" cake. Press Start.

148

Spiced Whipped Topping

Using the highest speed of your hand mixer, whisk together:
1 pint heavy whipping cream
½ Cup powdered sugar
½ tsp cinnamon
¼ tsp nutmeg

When thick, spread over the top of cooled cheesecake.

Sprinkle the remaining cinnamon on top and garnish with chocolate curls.

Return to refrigerator until ready to serve.

10. While Cheesecake is cooking, make the Whipped Topping recipe above.
11. When cooking time has elapsed, press Cancel and wait 30 minutes.
12. Remove cheesecake from pan, remove the foil (being careful not to get liquid onto the cheese cake) and refrigerate at least 3 hours.
13. To serve, open, expand and remove the exterior ring from the cheesecake.
14. Cover with Spiced Whipped Topping (below). Slice and enjoy!

TIP: MAKE A SLING OUT OF AN ALUMINUM FOIL STRIP (ABOUT 24" LONG AND DOUBLED FOR STRENGTH) TO PLACE UNDER THE SPRING FORM PAN TO AID IN REMOVAL OF HOT PAN.

Banana Nut Rice Pudding

Prep Time: 10 minutes Ready in: 15 minutes   Yield: 8 servings

INGREDIENTS
2 Cups long grain white rice
3 Tbsp butter
¼ Cup light, amber Agave Syrup
3 Cups water
3 Cups Milk
3 Tbsp sugar
1 tsp cinnamon
¼ tsp nutmeg
½ tsp imitation banana flavoring (Optional)
1/2 Cup half and half
1 Cup toasted pecan halves
2 fresh, ripe bananas

DIRECTIONS
1. Place your pressure cooker on a level surface, insert the pressure pot, and plug the unit in.
2. Set Cook Time for 8 minutes. Press Start
3. Add the rice, butter, Agave, water, milk, cinnamon and nutmeg to the pot stir well.
4. Attach the lid and turn the pressure valve to Air Tight.
5. Meanwhile, toast the pecan halves in the oven for 5-6 minutes at 350-F. Cool and coarsely chop.
6. When cooking time has elapsed, wait 5 minutes and release the remaining pressure manually.
7. Open the lid and carefully stir the rice. Stir in the banana flavoring and 1/2 Cup of half and half.
8. Attach lid to the pressure cooker, (set to Exhaust) or use Glass Lid. Let rest 5 minutes.
9. Stir well and serve hot with fresh banana slices, chopped toasted pecans and drizzle of Agave.
10. Refrigerate leftovers and serve cold or reheat in the microwave on the medium setting.

Note: pudding may need to be thinned with a little half and half if reheating.

HAWAIIAN BREAD PUDDING

Prep Time: 20 minutes   Ready in: 30 minutes   Yield: 8 servings

INGREDIENTS
8 Hawaiian sweet rolls
2 ¼ Cups milk
1 Tbsp butter
½ Cup brown sugar
¼ tsp salt
½ tsp cinnamon
½ tsp vanilla extract
¼ tsp rum extract (optional)
2 beaten eggs
¼ Cup dried mango
¼ Cup dried cranberries
¼ Cup dried pineapple

DIRECTIONS
1. Place pressure cooker onto a level surface, insert the pressure pot and plug in.
2. Grease the inside of a 2 quart oven safe bowl or dish that will fit inside the pressure cooker pot.
3. Prepare the bread by first cutting the browned top off and setting aside. Cut the bottom portion of the roll into quarters and place inside prepared dish.
4. Place the milk into a microwave safe dish and heat on high for 3 minutes. Add the butter, sugar, seasonings and extracts to the milk and stir completely.
5. Stir in the beaten egg and pour ¾ of the mixture over the bread cubes. Sprinkle ¾ of the dried fruit on top of the mixture. Arrange the tops of the rolls evenly across the top and pour on the remaining milk mixture and top with the remaining fruit. Cover the dish tightly with aluminum foil.
6. Place a low to-mid height rack into the cooker (or make a sling- see below) and pour 4 cups of hot water into the cooker. Place the sealed Bread Pudding onto the rack. Attach the lid and turn the pressure valve to Air Tight. Set Cook Time to 25 minutes and press Start.
7. When the cooking time has elapsed, turn the cooker off and let the cake remain inside for 10 minutes or until no pressure remains.   Carefully open the lid and remove the cake to a rack. Gently remove the foil.
8. Serve the pudding immediately with whipped cream, caramel sauce, toasted coconut or all by itself!   Store leftovers in the refrigerator.

TIP: MAKE A SLING BY TEARING OFF A PIECE OF FOIL, ABOUT 2 FEET LONG, AND FOLDING IT INTO THIRDS.
THIS SLING HELPS TO LOWER AND RAISE THE DISH IN AND OUT OF THE PRESSURE PAN.

LEMON CHEESECAKE
Prep Time: 15 minutes   Ready in: 4 hours   Yield: 8 servings

INGREDIENTS
6 graham crackers
1 Tbsp granulated sugar
4 Tbsp melted butter
1/4 tsp almond extract (optional)
1 1/2 Cups confectioners sugar
3 Tbsp cornstarch
1 tsp lemon zest
2 8-oz. blocks cream cheese at room temperature (do not use reduced fat varieties)
2 eggs at room temperature
4 Tbsp fresh lemon juice
1 1/2 Cups water
1 can of cherry, blueberry, or other fruit pie filling (optional)

DIRECTIONS
1. Generously butter bottom and sides of 8" (or the size that will fit into your pressure cooker) spring form pan.
2. Sprinkle graham cracker crumbs and sugar evenly on bottom of pan; drizzle butter overall. Lightly mix with fork and then press the mixture onto the bottom of the pan. Set pan aside.
3. In large mixing bowl, mix together cream cheese, confectioners sugar and cornstarch.
4. Beat in eggs, one at a time and then slowly drizzle in the lemon juice.
5. Pour batter into prepared springform pan. Cover top with wax paper and then completely cover entire pan with aluminum foil crimping top and bottom edges to seal out moisture.
6. Place your pressure cooker on a level surface, insert the pressure pan and plug in. Set Cook Time to 45 minutes and press Start. Pour the water into the cooker and center the steaming rack inside.
7. Place the covered cheesecake on top of the rack. Attach the lid and turn the pressure valve to Air Tight.
8. When the cooking time has elapsed, turn the cooker off and let the cake remain inside for 10 minutes or until no pressure remains. Carefully open the lid and remove the cake to a rack and gently remove the foil.
9. Serve warm within the next 20 minutes, at room temperature in about 45 minutes or cover with plastic wrap and place in the refrigerator to chill for at least 4 hours before serving.
10. To serve, gently run a thin knife around the edge of the cake before unlatching and removing the springform sides of the pan. Top with fresh fruit, glaze or cherry or blueberry pie filling (if desired), slice and serve.

Note: Store any leftovers in an air-tight container in the refrigerator or freeze for up to 6 months.

POACHED PEARS

Prep Time: 10 minutes   Ready in: 7 minutes   Yield: 1 pear per serving

INGREDIENTS
2-6 Pears
1 Cup Port Wine
2 cinnamon sticks
3 Tbsp butter
chocolate syrup
cool whip or home made whipped cream or ice cream

DIRECTIONS
1. Prepare the pears by peeling all but the very bottom and the very top of the pear.
2. Place your pressure cooker on a level surface, insert the pressure pot, and plug the unit in.
3. Set Cook Time for 7 minutes or press the Vegetable\Fish button and adjust. Press Start
4. Add the butter to the pot. When melted, add the port wine and cinnamon sticks and bring to a simmer.
5. Place the pears into the pot
6. Attach the lid and turn the pressure valve to Air Tight.
7. When cooking time has elapsed, wait 5 minutes and release the remaining pressure manually.
8. Open the lid and use tongs to serve the pears.
9. Top the pears with cool whip, chocolate, nuts or anything you desire!

THE HOT TARTNESS OF THE PEARS ARE PERFECT WITH THE COOLNESS OF WHIPPED CREAM
OR ICE CREAM. ADD A LITTLE CHOCOLATE SYRUP AND
OU HAVE A DELICIOUS, EASY DESSERT!

Chocolate Cherry Gooey Cake

Prep Time: 15 minutes   Ready in: 2 hours   Yield: 8 servings

INGREDIENTS
1 15.25 ounce triple chocolate fudge cake mix
1 cup water
¼ cup vegetable oil
3 large eggs
1 21 ounce can cherry pie filling; divided
2 Cups water

DIRECTIONS
1. Scoop 1/2 of the cherry pie filling into the bottom of a stainless steel mixing bowl; set aside.
2. In a large mixing bowl, combine the cake mix, water, oil and eggs and mix until smooth. Gently mix in the remaining pie filing until completely incorporated.
3. Pour the batter over the cherries in the mixing bowl.
4. Place your pressure cooker on a level surface, insert the pressure pan and plug in. Set Cook Time to 90 minutes and press Start. Pour 2 Cups water into the cooker and center the steaming rack inside.
5. Completely cover the top of the mixing bowl with alminum foil, pinching around the rim to keep the moisture out.
6. Place the covered bowl into the cooker; either on the rack or on the bottom if the mixing bowl has silicone on the bottom.
7. Attach the lid and turn the pressure valve to Air Tight.
8. When the cooking time has elapsed, turn the cooker off and let the cake remain inside for 10 minutes or until no pressure remains. Carefully open the lid and remove the cake to a rack and gently remove the foil.
9.   Serve warm within the next 20 minutes, at room temperature in about 45 minutes or cover with plastic wrap and place in the refrigerator to chill for at least 4 hours before serving.
10. To serve, gently run a thin knife around the edge of the cooked cake. Place plate over the top and invert the cake onto the plate.

STUFFED APPLES

Prep Time: 10 minutes   Ready in: 7 minutes   Yield: 1 apple per serving

INGREDIENTS

2-4 large apples; I use gala or fuji but any firm red apple will work

1/2 Cup dried cherries, cranberries or raisins
1/4 Cup brown sugar
1/4 pecans; chopped
1/2 tsp ground cinnamon

1 Cup apple juice
1 Tbsp butter

vanilla ice cream

DIRECTIONS

1. Prepare the apples by using a melon ball tool to hollow out the inside of the apple. The opening should be big enough to hold a little suffing but not too thin to become mushy.
2. Make the stuffing by tossing togehter the dried fruit, brown sugar, pecans and cinnamon. Place the stuffing into the hollows of the apples; set aside.
3. Place your pressure cooker on a level surface, insert the pressure pot, and plug the unit in.
4. Set Cook Time for 3 minutes or press the Vegetable\Fish button. Press Start
5. Add the butter to the pot and when melted, add the apple juice and bring to a simmer.
6. Place the apples into the pot
7. Attach the lid and turn the pressure valve to Air Tight.
8. When cooking time has elapsed, immediately release the pressure manually.
9. Open the lid and carefully use tongs to remove the apples. Serve with vanilla ice cream.

Pineapple Upside Down Cake

Prep Time: 10 minutes   Ready in: 1 hour   Yield: 8 servings

INGREDIENTS
¼ Cup light brown sugar
3 Tbsp butter
1 20-oz. can pineapple chunks; drained
1 10-oz. jar maraschino cherries; drained
1 pineapple cake mix prepared according to package directions

DIRECTIONS
1. Prepare the cake batter according to package directions.
2. Place pressure cooker onto a level surface, insert the pressure pot and plug in.
3. Set cook time for 40 minutes or select the Cake setting. Press Start.
4. Add the butter to the pot. When melted add the brown sugar, pineapple and cherries; stir until blended.
5. Pour the prepared cake batter over the fruit.
6. When cooking time has elapsed, let pressure release naturally.
7. Open the lid and allow to cool for 5-10 minutes before flipping onto a platter.

CINNAMON APPLE CAKE
Prep Time: 15 minutes   Ready in: 45 minutes   Yield: 8 servings

INGREDIENTS
1 15.25-ounce yellow cake mix
1 Cup water
1/3 Cup vegetable oil
3 large eggs

2 apples; 1 peeled and shredded (about 1 Cup) and the other cored and sliced on a mandolin
1 tsp cinnamon
2 Tbsp brown sugar

3 Tbsp butter
1/2 tsp cinnamon
1 Tbsp brown sugar

DIRECTIONS
1. In a large mixing bowl, combine the cake mix, water, oil and eggs and mix until smooth. Set batter aside.
2. Peel and shred the first apple and place into a measuring cup or small bowl. Toss in the cinnamon and the brown sugar until completely mixed. Set aside. Core and slice the second apple.
3. Place your pressure cooker on a level surface, insert the pressure pan and plug in. Set Cook Time to 30 minutes or select the Desserts button and press Start. Add butter to the pan.
4. When hot, add the sliced apples, 1/2 tsp cinnamon and 1 Tbsp brown sugar. Stir well to coat and then spread the slices in a single layer on the bottom.
5. Pour 1/2 of the cake batter over the apples. Layer on the shredded apple, brown sugar and cinnamon mixture; try to arrange the apples evenly and use any juice that may have formed.
6. Top with the remaining cake batter.
7. Attach the lid and turn the pressure valve to Air Tight.
8. When the cooking time has elapsed, turn the cooker off and let the cake remain inside for 10 minutes or until no pressure remains. Carefully open the lid. To serve, gently run a thin knife around the edge of the cooked cake. Place plate over the top and invert the cake onto the plate.

159

BLUEBERRY PEAR COBBLER
Prep Time: 15 minutes   Ready in: 40 minutes   Yield: 8 servings

INGREDIENTS
1 1/2 Cup self rising flour
1 1/2 Cup sugar
1 Cup milk
1/2 stick butter (4 Tbsp)

1 21-oz can Blueberry Pie Filling
2 pears; peeled, cored and sliced; use your apple slicer if you have one!
1 tsp cinnamon
2 Tbsp brown sugar

DIRECTIONS
1. In a large mixing bowl, combine the flour, sugar and milk; mix until smooth. Set batter aside.
2. Peel and slice the pears; toss in the cinnamon and the brown sugar until completely mixed. Set aside.
3. Place your pressure cooker on a level surface, insert the pressure pan and plug in. Set Cook Time to 18 minutes or select the Desserts button and press Start. Add the butter to the pan.
4. When hot, pour in the batter. Immediately top with the can of blueberry pie filling; even out the best you can.
5. Place the sliced pears in a decorative pattern across the top of the blueberry filling.
6. Attach the lid and turn the pressure valve to Air Tight.
7. When the cooking time has elapsed, turn the cooker off and let the cake remain inside for 10 minutes or until no pressure remains.
8. Carefully open the lid.
9. Serve with real whipped cream!

Tip: This is equally delicious using peaches and/or blackberries!

COCONUT RICE PUDDING
Prep Time: 10 minutes   Ready in: 15 minutes   Yield: 6 servings

INGREDIENTS
3 Cups jasmine rice
3 1/2 Cups water
3 Cans Thai Coconut Milk
2 7-oz bags Sunmaid® tropical trio dried fruit
1/4 Cup sugar
3 Tbsp butter
1/2 Cup Half n Half

DIRECTIONS
1. Place your pressure cooker on a level surface, insert the pressure pot, and plug the unit in.
2. Set Cook Time for 12 minutes or press the Rice button. Press Start
3. Add the rice, butter, water, sugar and coconut milk to the pot stir well. Stir in the dried fruit; save a little for garnish.
4. Attach the lid and turn the pressure valve to Air Tight.
5. Meanwhile, toast the coconut in the oven for 4-5 minutes at 350-F.
6. When cooking time has elapsed, wait 5 minutes and release the remaining pressure manually.
7. Open the lid and carefully stir the rice. Stir in the 1/2 Cup of half and half if needed to thicken.
8. Attach lid to the pressure cooker, (set to Exhaust) or use Glass Lid. Let rest 5 minutes.
9. Stir well and serve hot with toasted coconut.
10. Refrigerate leftovers and serve cold or reheat in the microwave on the medium setting.

Index

Index

Index

Index